Literary Origins of Surrealism

———

A New Mysticism in French Poetry

Original drawing by Yves Tanguy

Literary Origins of

SURREALISM

A New Mysticism in French Poetry

ANNA BALAKIAN

New York University Press

In Memory of
MY MOTHER
and
MY FATHER

Preface to the New Edition

THIS BOOK was first printed in 1947 under the aegis of the now defunct King's Crown Press of Columbia University. "It is," I wrote then, "with melancholy that I begin to write the foreword of a book started in the twilight months of peace, finished in the midst of war, printed over three years later." Today it is with nostalgia that I remember the wonderful people who had inspired me, those who had already disappeared by the time the book was published: Paul Hazard and Horatio Smith, and those of my mentors to whom I can renew my thanks: Jean-Albert Bédé and Justin O'Brien. I would also like to point out to a new generation of readers that at a time when study abroad was unthinkable this book would not have been possible without the precious documents that the Library of the Museum of Modern Art made freely available to me. *Literary Origins of Surrealism* cannot be separated from the marvelous frontispiece that the late Yves Tanguy created for it in that last period of his life which he spent in Conn., U.S.A., nor from the memory of the interview that André Breton gave me in his Greenwich Village apartment during his self-exile in America in World War II.

It is customary to apologize for an early work on the basis of the youth and inexperience that surrounded its gestation. Fortunately, in the case of poetry, whether one writes it or philosophizes about it, youth is an asset rather than a detriment, and inexperience can sometimes save one from a maze of "must" reference readings that clutter the bibliography without really contributing to the synthesis to which one aspires. Therefore, as I reread *Literary Origins of Surrealism,* I found to my amazement that there was no need to enlarge or "bring up to date" a bibliography which had in effect included only those books which served me directly in tracing the sources of surrealism. Although much has been written about surrealism itself since the first printing of this study, no revaluation seems to have been made of the origins of the movement nor has any new information come to light to shake the historical framework in which I placed the "new mysticism in French poetry." Maurice Nadeau's monumental history and compilation of surrealist documents had appeared the year before my work, but the break in communications between war-torn Europe and the U. S. was such that his two volumes did not reach me until two years later. Wallace Fowlie's *Age of Surrealism* (1950), which appeared a few years after my book, is a more generally readable work, but his stress was on interpretation of individual surrealist writers rather than on the philosophical and poetic concepts which predated surrealism and contributed to it. More recently, Roger Shattuck in *The Banquet Years* (1958) has studied the early years of the present century for their own intrinsic worth rather than in terms of their function as aesthetic ancestry for surrealism.

It has been a source of surprise to me that *Literary Origins of Surrealism* has been considered primarily as a study of surrealism. Perhaps because so little was known about literary surrealism in this country at the time, and so few of the works were available in the original, much less in translation, the book was read particularly for what it could contribute to the understanding of surrealism and its immediate antecedent, dadaism. Today, surrealist and dada documentations and studies, as well as their subsequent effects on avant-garde movements all over the world, have made these literary schools much better known.

I hope that this new edition may direct attention to the book's chapters on Baudelaire, Rimbaud, Lautréamont, and Mallarmé. I had tried to draw Rimbaud out of the spiritualized commentaries that had made him a sounding board for the critics' erudition and psychological speculations. I had hoped to bring light to one of Mallarmé's major works, *Igitur,* which at the time was so little known, and to introduce Lautréamont to American readers. In short, I had attempted to take these three writers out of the mainstream of symbolist history and to observe them in a different orbit. As for Baudelaire, I had felt that "Les Correspondences" was overrated as a doctrinal poem, and that Baudelaire's prose works needed more study in terms of their contribution to the avant-garde. Baudelaire seemed to me more hybrid and complex an author than he had been deemed by the historians of symbolism; I wanted to demonstrate the validity of André Breton's contention that all modern poetry begins with Baudelaire's "Le Voyage." Today I have come to realize that even in "Les Correspondences" Baudelaire is not as symbolist as it has been assumed, and that if he paraphrases Swedenborgian duality in the first part of the poem, the last part of the sonnet contradicts the beginning and deviates from symbolism; in this light Baudelaire now appears to me even more of a modernist in his concept of nature and his mystical approach to reality than when I wrote this book.

The principal aim of *Literary Origins of Surrealism* had been to extract the lineage of surrealism from among the poetic miscellany of the second half of the nineteenth century in France. In today's broadened comparative view of literature I send "la bouteille à la mer" again for what direction it may be able to give to those who transcend the frontiers between native and foreign literatures, a particularly difficult feat in the case of poetry, where translation is often of less help than first-hand commentary on the original materials.

ANNA BALAKIAN

August 1965
Babylon, N. Y.

Contents

Introduction

THE RELATION of Surrealism to the social and psychological revolt of the first "post war" period, as revealed by its deep antipathy for bourgeois society, has already been treated in connection with the history of the poetic thought of the past seventy-five years in France.[1] Surrealism has been regarded as a stylistic revolution, as a study in neuropathology, as an aftermath of the "dérèglement des sens" suggested by Rimbaud some fifty years earlier. The precursors of the Surrealists have been indicated not only by historians of literature, but by the Surrealists themselves.[2] A long line of writers have been linked because of their rejection of the same kind of literature and art, and because of their parallel adventures in the world of the "merveilleux" and the unknown.

My motive in exploring once more the pathways leading from Romanticism to Baudelaire, and from Baudelaire to Lautréamont, Rimbaud and Mallarmé, down to the nihilism of Dada, is to attempt to show that these writings have contributed not so much to each other as to one general revolution in poetic mysticism; that this change, finding expression in a fusion of poetry with prose, has not only affected the *form* of art but has developed a new philosophy of reality which has been shaping around materialism the mystical propensity of a considerable number of twentieth-century artists.

The tremendous mystical motivation beneath the surrealist texts is evident; and it is obvious that they are the product of a craving for the unknown; but what makes for the difference between the *invisible* of the Romanticists and the *reality* of the Surrealists? Has the craving for the unknown simply become more acute because modern scientific dis-

1. The most important of these works is Marcel Raymond's *De Baudelaire au surréalisme*.
2. See André Breton's *Manifeste du surréalisme*; Tristan Tzara, "Essai sur la situation de la poésie," *Le Surréalisme au Service de la Révolution*, IV, 15; André Breton, "Qu'est-ce que le surréalisme?".

coveries have cleared more and more of the mysteries of the physical world? Has the folklore legend given way to a more appropriate medium for the exploration of *the strange*, such as simulation of insanity or dreams? Or, rather, has this unusual mysticism brought about a new technique of representation which makes the strange world of Romanticists like Hoffmann or Arnim seem quite familiar and acceptable to the imagination of the reader in contrast with a poem by Breton or a picture by Tanguy.

In the evolution of the art of linguistic representation of the "merveilleux," both a breaking down process and a building up process can be observed: the breaking down process is connected with the artist's changing concept of *nature*, while the building up process might be associated with the cultivation of a new state of mind, called in turn, "inconscient," "subconscient," "irrationnel," and culminating in a new logic based on the linking together and acceptance of contradictory entities. This was basically a reaction to the imitation of nature in art and literature; taking its roots in the escapism of the Romanticists, this anti-naturalism became a strong element of the spiritual crisis of 1870, and directed the eye of the artist toward the discovery of an "inconnu nouveau."[3] Finally, dissatisfaction with halfway measures and the adaptation of old technique to new perspectives led to the demolition work of Dadaism, which was to be based on the notion that an object or a phenomenon could continue to exist when freed of its natural framework.

The critics from 1870 to the appearance of Dada showed a tendency to classify all the poetic product of their contemporaries into the literary schools which self-conscious poet-theorists had established without clear definitions. For instance, the orderly, classical dreams of a Kahn or a Régnier—whose poetic dream perceptions were as normal, once the mental transition was made from the real to the imaginary, as their actual sensations—were classed side by side, in the name of symbolism, with the extraordinary visions of a Rimbaud. The reason given for this classification is expediency. In his *Symbolistes et Décadents*, Gustave Kahn, fully aware of the inadequacy of the word "symbolism," characterizes it as a convenient word used to include many new poetic elements, recognized but not yet defined:

3. Louis Aragon, *La Peinture au défi*; "L'évasion de Rimbaud se perd dans un inconnu nouveau. Elle résume et nie ce qui la précède," p. 7.

Le mot symbolisme avait pris dès lors (1886-9) sa carrure et son sens. Ce n'était pas qu'il fût très précis, mais il est bien difficile de trouver un mot qui caractérise bien des efforts différents, et symbolisme valait à tout prendre romantisme.[4]

The bulk of the poets grouped by Kahn, Moréas, Mendès and others as "symbolists" will be omitted in this study; theirs was on the whole a process of dressing reality with extra trappings rather than the denuding of poetry which led to the concept of surreality.[5]

Symbolism developed several generations of writers, underwent many subdivisions, but it was not until after 1910, when a certain perspective made it possible to envisage the poetry of the preceding decades over and above poetic schools, that poets began to be freed of arbitrary classifications, and that a critical evaluation of each work based on a closer scrutiny was attempted. It was at a time when the subconscious and the problems of the real and the unreal came into vogue that these very phases were noted in the poets of the period which had thus far been named merely symbolist or decadent. André Barre in his study of Symbolism is one of the first to point to a certain predilection for the "unreal" among some of the Symbolists. Moreover, the profound study of Albert Thibaudet on Mallarmé in 1911 and Jacques Rivière's illuminating articles on Rimbaud and on Dadaism in the *Nouvelle Revue Française* in 1914 and 1920 respectively, are among the first to indicate clearly in certain of the "symbolists" something besides symbolism. Rivière noticed that underneath the theories and terminologies of recent literary schools there were evidences of an important change in the attitude of the writer of the last hundred years toward exterior reality:

> Il faudra tâcher un jour de décrire en détail, et avec illustrations à l'appui, la lente modification qui s'est produite au cours du XIXe siècle dans l'attitude mentale de l'écrivain. En gros, elle a consisté dans un progressif affaiblissement de l'instinct objectif, dans une foi de plus en plus grêle à l'importance des modèles extérieurs, dans

---

4. G. Kahn, *Symbolistes et Décadents,* pp. 51-2.
5. The Surrealists' hostility toward excessive symbolism is pointedly expressed in René Crevel's treatise on poetry: "La poésie qui nous délivre des symboles plante la liberté elle-même et son ascension laisse très loin derrière, très bas sous elle, les sons, les couleurs qui l'expriment. Mais quel technicien comprendra jamais?" *L'Esprit contre la raison.* See also T. Tzara, "Essai," p. 18.

un détachement croissant de la realité, et conjointement dans une identification de plus en plus étroite du sujet avec lui-même. . . .[6]

But it was primarily after the early Surrealists (many of whom proved better critics than poets) had claimed certain Symbolists as their precursors, that these were found to have qualities other than a vague newness in thought and in form.

A new classification was gradually attempted. François Ruchon in his study of Rimbaud in 1927 sees in him the first signs of a new lyricism: "Avec Lautréamont, avec Rimbaud et, après eux, avec Mallarmé et Laforgue, s'est constituée une nouvelle forme du lyrisme, un lyrisme ésotérique, tourné vers l'intérieur, anti-social."[7] In the same year Jacques Maritain observes in the artistic product of the last half century a revolution comparable to that of the Renaissance: "On dirait que depuis un demi-siècle un autre accès d'introspection s'est emparé de lui [i.e. l'art], donnant lieu à une révolution au moins aussi importante."[8] At this same time Marcel Raymond in his synthesis of poetry from Baudelaire to the Surrealists places Rimbaud, Mallarmé, Lautréamont, Jarry, Saint-Pol-Roux, and Maeterlinck on a higher level than the rest of the Symbolists and points to their influence on later poets. The emphasis changes. More and more citations are made that would tend to reveal the poet's hatred of reality and his desire to flee from it. In *Initiation à la littérature d'aujourd'hui* (1928), Emile Bouvier calls the "poètes maudits": "les grands affranchis." He sees in Rimbaud not a dreamer but a creator of a reality which he calls "supraterrestre."[9] He believes that art has gradually become "un procédé d'évasion,"[10] and that invention has become the task of the artist. To arrive at a definition of this "invention" it will be necessary to take as a point of departure the present aspects of Surrealism.

At the beginning of this investigation it appeared, at first glance, that a conclusive picture could be drawn within the time limits of 1870 and 1920. However, earlier traces of this change in the mysticism of the French poet came to light. On the other hand, certain influences

6. Jacques Rivière, "Reconnaissance à Dada," *Nouvelle Revue Française*, XV (1ᵉʳ août, 1920), 225.

7. F. Ruchon, *J. A. Rimbaud*, p. 260.

8. J. Maritain, "Frontières de la poésie," *Le Roseau d'or*, no. 3.

9. E. Bouvier, *Initiation à la littérature d'aujourd'hui*, p. 43.

10. *Ibid.*, p. 189.

believed to exist between the German Romanticists and the French poets of the end of the nineteenth century were found to be totally misleading in relation to the present study and had to be shown as negative factors. Moreover, it proved arbitrary to stop at the very first manifestations of the Surrealist school. It is true that, from the first, surrealist texts embody characteristics and tendencies developed in the course of the last hundred years; but it seemed more advisable to begin this study with an analysis of those salient elements of Surrealism which have survived the more violent character of the earliest manifestoes, and then to show the evolution of these ideas and techniques.

CHAPTER I

Surreality

D'abord, un grand désir m'était venu de solennité et d'apparat. J'avais froid. Tout mon être vivant et corrompu aspirait à la majesté des morts. Je fus tenté ensuite par un mystère où les formes ne jouent aucun rôle. Curieux d'un ciel décoloré d'où les oiseaux et les nuages sont bannis. Je devins esclave de la faculté pure de voir, esclave de mes yeux irréels et vierges, ignorant du monde et d'eux-mêmes. Puissance tranquille. Je supprimai le visible et l'invisible, je me perdis dans un miroir sans tain. Indestructible, je n'étais pas aveugle.[11]

FIRST a desire for death in all its natural, majestic manifestations; then the temptation proffered by a new mystery made up of the emptiness of a sky that has been denuded of its external attributes and is envisaged by senses freed of their past perceptions; then the will to suppress not only the visible but that which man's mind has for so long relegated to the realm of the imperceptible that it has thereby been robbed of existence; last, the loss of one's personality in a mirror that will absorb the already known image. And the poet will experience a new vision, not with his human sight, but with new eyes which are one with his indestructibility. . . .

This passage from Paul Eluard's *Les Dessous d'une vie ou la Pyramide humaine* has been chosen as the point of departure for this study, and paraphrased, because in the concise framework of this brief adventure in the realm of the surreal are represented all the steps which Eluard and his contemporaries, advancing in the direction indicated by several generations of French poets, have taken to create the state of being and writing which they term surreality. This brief excerpt, so totally devoid of natural imagery, reflects the Surrealists' rejection of a world in which light and dark, the real and the unreal, the living and

11. P. Eluard, *Les Dessous d'une vie ou la Pyramide humaine*, p. 13.

the dead, are regarded as contradictory entities. How they have arrived at this concept is the subject to be treated.

In an interview in October, 1941, André Breton stated that the following traits continued to remain essential in surrealist activity:[12] alienation of sensation, the deep exploration of "objective hazard"— the term used by the Surrealists to describe the unpredictable and seemingly illogical forces which control the succession of events—and "the great modern tradition," as he put it, which originated from Baudelaire's:

> *Plonger au fond du gouffre, Enfer ou Ciel qu'importe!*
> *Au fond de l'Inconnu pour trouver du nouveau!*

These, then, are the characteristics that remain of all the manifestoes, psycho-physiological theories, exhibitionism, questionnaires, table-turning, willful dreaming and journalistic anarchy of the twenties.[13] But the qualities which have survived are not the exclusive property of Surrealism: they are the crystallization of a historical and artistic development which, appearing on the surface to be a form of poetic escapism, became more and more exigent and evolved into a new concept of art. As Albert Thibaudet aptly stated: "Il y a eu, longtemps après Rimbaud et Lautréamont, une révolution rimbaldienne et maldororale, pour laquelle nous pouvons choisir ce titre que les manuels donnent à l'histoire de la fin du XVe siècle: la Découverte des Mondes Nouveaux."[14] What are we to look for in tracing the steps in this discovery of New Worlds? The answer depends on the motivation behind this alienation of sensation, this deep exploration of hazard, and the insatiable quest for the unknown.

First, why the insatiable quest for the unknown? The reason has been given many a time in the poetry of the last hundred years. The poet has long been represented as a captive trying to tear down his prison walls; the poet is the "dreamer among the ramparts" in Pierre Reverdy's modern interpretation of the old image. But the walls have gradually taken on a more dreary aspect and, for the Surrealists, encompass the whole range of human experience. They mark the limits of the dream rather than those of reality. It is beyond these barriers that reality lies: "Où

12. See "Interview with André Breton," *View,* October-November 1941, p. 2.

13. See Surrealist periodicals: *Littérature, Révolution Surréaliste, Le Surréalisme au Service de la Revolution.*

14. A. Thibaudet, "Révolution des cinq," *Revue de Paris,* 15 août, 1934, p. 806.

les sens sont souverains la réalité s'efface, s'évanouit. Le naturalisme est un exemple de cette soumission à la réalité sensible."[15] The surrealist movement opens with a grim realization that these walls that block the artist's vision are unshakable. In the earliest manifestation of surrealistic writing, *Les Champs magnétiques* (1920), the basic note is, therefore, that of despair: despite all the joys, all the landscapes, all the knowledge brought within the grasp of humanity, the poet regrets living in the organized world, and at the same time he sees little hope of finding an outlet:

LA GLACE SANS TAIN

Prisonniers des gouttes d'eau, nous ne sommes que des animaux perpétuels. Nous courons dans les villes sans bruits et les affiches enchantées ne nous touchent plus. A quoi bon ces grands enthousiasmes fragiles, ces sauts de joie desséchés. Nous ne savons plus rien que les astres morts. . . . Notre bouche est plus sèche que les plages perdues; nos yeux tournent sans but, sans espoir. . . . Les gares merveilleuses ne nous abritent plus jamais. . . . Il faut donc étouffer encore pour vivre ces minutes plates, ces siècles en lambeaux. Nous aimions autrefois les soleils de fin d'année, les plaines étroites où nos regards coulaient comme ces fleuves impétueux de notre enfance. Il n'y a plus que des reflets dans ces bois repeuplés d'animaux absurdes, de plantes connues. Un jour dont on ne sait plus la couleur, nous avons découvert des murs tranquilles et plus forts que les monuments. . . . Il n'y avait plus que la mort ingrate qui nous respectait. Chaque chose est à sa place, et personne ne peut plus parler: chaque sens se paralysait et des aveugles étaient plus dignes que nous.[16]

Thus spoke André Breton and Philippe Soupault, finding themselves unable even to *breathe* in a world that had lost all life for them. And there is no physical flight: "Itinéraires interrompus et tous les voyages terminés."[16] In the orderly world where the very things they once loved have shaped a prison, they are left to face bluntly their tremendous despair: "L'immense sourire de toute la terre ne nous a pas suffi. . . . Ce plat ferait bon effet sur toutes les tables. C'est dommage que nous n'ayons plus faim."[16]

15. P. Reverdy, "Le Rêveur parmi les murailles," *Révolution Surréaliste*, I, 20.

16. A. Breton, P. Soupault, *Les Champs Magnétiques*, pp. 9-17.

Nor has Science given any real satisfaction to the seekers of a greater reality: according to the Surrealist René Crevel, "La Déesse Science' has proved a great disappointment although everyone pretends to think her capable of illuminating the secrets of man.[17] Philosophy, too, has misled the seeker of the absolute; the Surrealists see it merely as the history of the ideas which hold humanity confined to a "petite réalité exploitable."[18]

But what shuts off from our view a greater reality? Physical nature, which Crevel calls the "bric-à-brac réaliste"[19] and the positivist turn of mind which accepts it as complete reality! The mission of the poet who has inherited this bric-a-brac is to rise above it by combatting the realistic attitude which is a sure symptom of mediocrity.[20]

The word "nature," which for centuries had been used synonymously with reality, is now used to designate merely the exterior world; in Louis Aragon's words: "Je m'avouai ne pas trouver l'ombre de raison à ce sens partitif du mot nature. Je ne l'employai plus que pour signifier d'un coup le monde extérieur."[21] In his lecture on "Painting and Reality," Aragon shows how the rivalry of photography, which could represent nature so much more accurately than art, finally caused the artist to be dissatisfied with imitation and drove him to a competition with nature. Nature is no longer considered the "supreme good," and the artist today finds it quite possible to throw off the "naturalistic illusion" and to become the "master of nature"; as a matter of fact, he would not know how else to exercise his art.[22] Thus speaks Aragon quite simply and states, as a fact, what took a long line of poets and artists more than fifty years to accept as one of their most fundamental aims. It is the result of a long struggle to abandon the Romantic devotion of an earlier age to the exterior manifestations of nature and the habit of turning the known forms of nature into the symbols of the poet's mysticism. This "mania," which consists in reducing the unknown entity to the level of the known and in classifying it, handicaps, according to Breton, the seeker of the infinite, the absolute, the eternal.[23]

17. R. Crevel, *L'Esprit contre la raison,* p. 13.
18. *Ibid.,* p. 21.
19. *Ibid.,* p. 39.
20. A. Breton, *Manifeste du surréalisme,* p. 16.
21. L. Aragon, *Le Paysan de Paris,* p. 152.
22. L. Aragon, *Painting and Reality,* pp. 7-10.
23. A. Breton, *op. cit.,* p. 20.

The dominant characteristic of this exterior nature and of the state of mind which classifies and simplifies is *order* and the mental activity based on order, i.e. logical thinking. This, according to the Surrealists, is adequate only in dealing with minor problems.[24] Hence the revolt is not really directed against the world of matter, against the concrete, but against the mode of grasping concrete matter, i.e. through reason and rational thinking based on the concept of order, whether it be in perceiving nature or in imagining the "unreal" of eternity. We have but to look at some of the titles of the works of Surrealists to see how united they are in their fervor to free thought from reason: *Antitête, Etes-vous fou?, L'Esprit contre la raison, Alphabet sourd aveugle, Défense de savoir, L'Impossible.* And *Nadja,* the most important of Breton's works, is an attempt to create a character freed from the natural order of things and living in its own orbit of reality. Imagination, thus breaking the bars of its "cage raisonnable," attempts to realize the dream of Mallarmé and his contemporaries.[25]

Thus we find the Surrealist looking with contempt upon the exterior world. He refuses to follow the contours of objects and the succession of events.[26] He chides man for his blindness and deafness and muteness.[27] While this mysticism possesses in common with Christian mysticism the tendency to seek and value the eternal aspects of existence, it entails an entirely different concept of the eternal. The Surrealist regards the Christian concept of the infinite and that of the pantheist as a complete failure. According to him, Christian and pantheistic philosophy keep humanity as fully imprisoned in the external world as naturalism or realism. For, as the Surrealist sees it: "l'homme a toujours lié ses représentations divines à l'image du corps humain."[28] In a more derisive manner, Victor Crastre compares our representations of the divine to manikins, describes them as pure imitations of nature: "L'absolu, leur terreur, ils l'ont appelé Dieu . . . Dieu et société ne font qu'un. Ce n'est qu'au delà de Dieu que l'on peut créer un monde nouveau : avec lui nous devons engager une lutte au couteau."[29] The crystallization of the concept

---

24. Both Breton and a few years later Crevel express this idea in identical words: see Breton, *op. cit.,* p. 21 and Crevel, *L'Esprit contre la raison,* p. 45.

25. R. Crevel, *ibid.,* p. 47.

26. *Ibid.,* p. 36.

27. P. Eluard, *"En Société,"* *Les Dessous d'une vie,* p. 76.

28. L. Aragon, *Le Paysan de Paris,* p. 187.

29. Victor Crastre, *"Invention de Dieu,"* *Révolution Surréaliste,* VI, 28-29.

of the infinite into a concept of a god prevents man, according to the Surrealists, from further prodding and from being on the alert for further discoveries; instead, it holds him a prisoner. Innumerable are the Surrealist works proclaiming this attitude toward religion, glorifying this mystically inspired atheism. In an article "Athéisme et Révolution," Maxime Alexandre, a contributor to the *Surréalisme au Service de la Révolution,* expresses very clearly the general opinion: "L'esprit religieux, c'est-à-dire, cet ensemble de sentiments et d'idées qui tendent à maintenir l'homme prisonnier de lui-même et des autres hommes. . . ."[30] Belief in God is associated in their minds with a certain smugness, an assurance of another world which will answer our longing for the infinite; while waiting for this other world, man is seen holding a terrified respect for the Church, a reverence which robs him of his liberty of investigation here on earth. That is what prompts Crevel to speak of "Dieu et ses murs,"[31] and to disdainfully call God "président des compagnies d'assurance sur l'Eternité."[32] The real mystic, according to him, would not seek the protection of the haven that is God, in his voyage toward the infinite; he turns away from this haven, crying: "que m'importe un *ailleurs* que je ne saurais imaginer assez différent de cet *ici.*"[33]

The only god the Surrealists accept is their own image of the inconceivable. Humanity is constantly evaluating all phenomena in the world according to the standards of *order* and then finding the "merveilleux" and the "mystérieux" within the bounds of this order, as a result of its own endeavors at simplification. The inconceivable, therefore, according to the Surrealists, is *disorder.* Thus, disorder becomes the real god; and Providence which is generally revered as the manifestation of the mystical order of things, gives way to the worship of *hazard,* or chance, the mystical manifestation of the inconceivable but existent *disorder* of things. That is why we find Aragon saying: "Je vivais au hasard, à la poursuite du hasard, qui seul parmi les divinités avait su garder son prestige."[34] That is how Paul Eluard finds a mystical revelation in what, to the average reader, would seem a purpose-

---

30. M. Alexandre, *Le Surréalisme au Service de la Révolution,* I, 41.
31. R. Crevel, *Le Clavecin de Diderot,* pp. 64-8.
32. R. Crevel, *Etes-vous fou?,* pp. 214-5.
33. *Ibid.,* p. 213.
34. L. Aragon, *Le Paysan de Paris,* p. 139.

less coincidence, when he discovers that objective hazard has arranged the printed form of Tristan Tzara's *Grains et Issues* in such a way as to have six consecutive lines begin with the letter "p."[35] In the light of the importance that the Surrealists attach to "hazard," expressions such as the two above are not tongue-in-the-cheek poses but the fruit of profound convictions, developed through a long period of poetic activity. It was the germs of this same conviction that prompted Mallarmé to say: "Un coup de dés jamais n'abolira le hasard"; for what is the "coup de dés" but the will of man; what is "hasard" from the point of view of Mallarmé and of those who followed in his footsteps but the irrational, disorderly will of the universe! And it was this same worship of hazard which drove the Dadaists to seek in "collage"[36] a new reality. As a matter of fact, it is by extracting this "divine" disorder left so long undisturbed in concrete entities that the Surrealists will hope to perceive the concrete face of the infinite instead of giving in to the initial despair which assailed them. "Le concret du désordre serait la limite absolue de l'esprit,"[37] states Aragon. The concrete form of this disorder is what he is looking for in *Le Paysan de Paris* when he says: "Je me suis mis à découvrir le visage de l'infini sous les formes concrètes qui m'escortaient, marchant le long des allées de la terre,"[38] and not the *order* that a deist, saying exactly the same thing, would have been seeking. It is this same concrete form of disorder that Breton has represented in creating Nadja, "une étoile au cœur même du fini."[39] Here lies the ideal of all the Surrealists, and, as we shall see, it was this same image that Rimbaud, Lautréamont, Mallarmé, had been seeking.

We are thus dealing with a cumulative poetic indictment of that type of human thought which has chosen to place heaven outside of the reach of the material world; poetic it is, and passionate! "Ils ont mis le ciel ailleurs. Ils ont oublié mes yeux en imaginant les étoiles."[40] But this indictment is not limited to religion; it is also

---

35. See footnote to the preface by P. Eluard to Mesens' *Alphabet sourd aveugle.*

36. A form of amusement (or of art according to Dada) which consisted of cutting up newspaper items, shuffling them in a hat, drawing them out and pasting them one after the other according to the divine "hazard" that controlled the order of their appearance.

37. L. Aragon, *op. cit.,* p. 236.

38. *Ibid.,* pp. 142-3.

39. A. Breton, *Nadja,* p. 206.

40. L. Aragon, *op. cit.,* p. 250.

directed toward chemistry, physiology, and other branches of learning, which Aragon groups under the term of "les psychologies." Both religion and science are to the Surrealist outlets of the positivist attitude of mind which shuts the door to a daring exploration of the surreal: ". . . L'homme en face de tout abîme apprenait à connaître les parois de l'abîme, et les tourments de l'infini. Irréductible positivisme humain."[41]

It will be seen in the following chapters that this disdainful attitude toward scientific progress and this total confusion as to the meaning of religion are not sudden manifestations. They are essential traits of an entire poetic lineage, as the Surrealists themselves have often indicated. And yet, ironically, this poetry borrowed from science and religion the most fundamental characteristics of each: from religion the "aile,"[42] the desire to transcend ordinary life, and from science the method of untiring objective investigation, experimentation, coöperative activity, and collective discovery: "Le merveilleux doit être fait par tous et non point par un seul,"[43] says Louis Aragon, as he traces back to Lautréamont this conscious loss of individualism in art.

The subject of this poetico-scientific investigation is the effort of the mind to liberate itself, as we have seen, from the process of logical thought which, according to the Surrealists, cannot grasp nor express the divine disorder. Reason has betrayed the Mind;[44] now the mind must find ways of freeing itself of reason. If it succeeds, it will at last strike correctly the strings of the clavichord of the senses.[45] The Surrealists must, therefore, investigate the recesses of the mind barred by reason. This means that they must first of all recognize the discoveries already made along this line by those who came before them. By going as far back as the Romanticists, Tristan Tzara gives in an issue of *Le Surréalisme au Service de la Révolution* a rather conclusive list of what he and his contemporaries have found in some of the poetry of the nineteenth century; the cult of the phantom,

41. Aragon, *op. cit.*, p. 192.

42. As Aragon writes in *Le Paysan de Paris*, p. 193: "Ce que je sais d'un dieu, moi le bronze, ce que je sais du Dieu pressenti, c'est l'aile et puisqu'il paraît qu'on l'implore, c'est l'aile que nous implorons, du piédestal où nous sommes pétrifiés, de cet embarcadère sans bateau, d'où nous tendons nos mains vers l'inconnaissable."

43. L. Aragon, *La Peinture au défi*, p. 29.

44. See R. Crevel, *Le Clavecin de Diderot*, p. 47; also *L'Esprit contre la raison*.

45. Crevel, *Le Clavecin de Diderot*, p. 147.

magic, vice (sexual liberty),[46] the dream, insanity, passion, folklore,[47] and real and imaginary voyage.[48] In examining certain poetic works of the nineteenth century, an attempt will be made to determine to what extent these subjects were exploited by the Romanticists and their successors with the same motive and results as the Surrealists, that of exploring the divine disorder.

But while the Surrealists were familiarizing themselves with these poetic discoveries of the nineteenth century, they came at the same time upon a scientific work which synchronized perfectly with the development of the new poetic attitude: this was the study made by Dr. Jean-Martin Charcot of hysteria. Indeed by 1928 the Surrealists are celebrating the "Fiftieth Anniversary of Hysteria" and calling the work of Charcot the greatest poetic discovery of the nineteenth century.[49]

Charcot had not been, of course, the first to experiment on cases of hysteria.[50] However, his work had attracted the attention of both layman and scientist to a far greater extent than that of his predecessors since the publication of his findings had been accompanied by an iconography, edited by his colleague Bourneville and an expert photographer, P. Regnard. This *Iconographie de la Salpêtrière* had been worked out between 1875 and 1880, and publication had begun in 1878. It is the anniversary of this particular document that the Surrealists, under the influence of Breton, were celebrating in 1928.[51] As Breton himself had practiced medicine and had been particularly interested

46. The parenthesis is Tzara's.

47. In his *Manifeste du surréalisme,* André Breton points to the folklore legend and particularly to that of children's fairy tales as being akin to surrealist activity. He deplores the fact that children are too soon immunized to the marvelous charm of legend: "De bonne heure ceux-ci sont sevrés de merveilleux, et, plus tard, ne gardent pas une assez grande virginité d'esprit pour prendre un plaisir extrême à *Peau d'âne"* (p. 30). He wishes there were such stories for adults: ". . . l'homme croirait déchoir à se nourrir de contes de fées. . . . Il y a des contes à écrire pour les grandes personnes, des contes encore presque bleus (pp. 30-1). In the chapter on Rimbaud I shall try to point out how indeed one child did not too soon become insensible to this form of the "merveilleux" and in effect tried to utilize this element in his deviation from nature.

48.T. Tzara, "Essai sur la Situation de la Poésie," *Le Surréalisme au Service de la Révolution,* IV, 16.

49. L. Aragon, A. Breton, "Le Cinquantenaire de l'Hystérie," *Révolution Surréaliste,* 4ᵉ année, XI, 20.

50. Braid, Berheim, and Liebeault had been the immediate precursors of Charcot; these in turn had been disciples of Mesmer. See Margaret Goldsmith, *Franz Anton Mesmer,* London, Barker, 1934.

51. The article appearing in the *Révolution Surréaliste,* was illustrated with reproductions of photographs taken at the Salpêtrière.

in mental disorders, he was well acquainted with Charcot's laboratory of the Salpêtrière.

Charcot had been the link between medicine and art. What Breton and his followers had sensed in the poetic expression of the latter part of the nineteenth century, Charcot seemed to have confirmed in his observation of clinical cases: that it was possible for the human mind to conciliate objective reality with the dream and to experience this conciliation without exterior stimuli or artificial hypnosis:

> Il est des sujets, et peut-être sont-ils plus nombreux qu'on ne le pense, chez qui la plupart des manifestations tant psychiques que somatiques de l'hypnotisme peuvent se rencontrer à l'état de veille, sans qu'il soit nécessaire de faire intervenir les pratiques d'hypnotisation. Il semble que l'état hypnotique qui, pour d'autres, est un état artificiel, soit pour ces singulières créatures, l'état ordinaire, l'état normal, si tout est qu'en pareille circonstance, il puisse être question d'état normal. Ces gens-là, passez-moi le mot, *dorment,* alors même qu'ils semblent parfaitement éveillés; ils procèdent, en tout cas, dans la vie commune ainsi que dans un songe, plaçant sur le même plan la réalité objective et le rêve qu'on leur impose, vu tout au moins, entre les deux, ils ne font guère de différence.[52]

The photographs of hysterics (which moved the Surrealists so deeply!) expressed attitudes similar to those of the saints and the "possessed" of the Middle Ages: their passionate movements, their simulation of crucifixion, their exaltation. Moreover, the descriptions of the hallucinations given by the doctors of La Salpêtrière were amazingly reminiscent of the confessions of nuns of Loudun and Louvier. The miracles of the Middle Ages, the visions of angels and demons are all considered by Charcot and his co-workers as manifestations of the same type of hysteria as noticed in the inmates of La Salpêtrière: ". . . Les attitudes qu'elles prennent font songer aux attitudes sous lesquelles on représente les mystiques du Moyen Age, les Saintes les plus renommées par leur exaltation religieuse."[53] Thus, ordinary women seemed subjected to the same unusual visions

52. J. M. Charcot, *Leçons sur les maladies du système nerveux*, III, 336.
53. Bourneville, Regnard, *Iconographie photographique de la Salpêtrière,* (Service Charcot), I, 107-8, *Aux Bureaux du Progrès Médical,* 1876-80.

that had been considered heretofore the power of religious fanatics. It seemed that Charcot had been showing through his scientific study of hysteria the same "matérialisation du miracle"[54] which was being essayed in poetry. Moreover, Charcot had indicated that hysteria was not confined to the clinic only, that cases of hysteria were more frequent than had previously been thought. He had especially pointed out that cases of hysteria could be found among men, as well as women.[55] He had, furthermore, emphasized its particular prevalence in the latter part of the nineteenth century. Thus, if it were not such a rare state, it could be simulated by the sane and used as a means of expression. Attracted by the strange, hallucinated expression of these photographed cases, Breton and Aragon insisted that: "L'hystérie n'est pas un phénomène pathologique et peut, à tous égards, être considérée comme un moyen d'expression."[56]

Not only hysteria but all forms of insanity would be worth imitating, since the power of insanity was "au-dessus de l'humain"[57] just as the exaltation of the hysteric person was greater, they thought, than that of the average Christian mystic. As a matter of fact, an examination of some of the cases of insanity reported by Dr. Charcot in his *Leçons sur les maladies du système nerveux*, shows expressions of the same sort of disorder that the Surrealists were later to attempt. For instance, there is the case of the verbal blindness of a patient who said: "j'ai une main dans le soleil,"[58] substituting one word for another and accepting this disorder as reality. It is, therefore, not surprising to find Breton and Eluard saying in *L'Immaculée Conception*: "à nos yeux l'essai de simulation de maladie qu'on enferme remplacerait avantageusement la ballade, le sonnet, l'épopée, le poème sans queue ni tête et autres genres caducs."[59] It is not intended here to enter into an analysis of these numerous simulations attempted by Breton, Eluard, and others; what interests us is that these constitute an intensification of the same type of conscious alienation of sensations that we shall find attempted by Lautréamont and Rimbaud, and which are opposed in character to the literary expression which Hoelderlin and Nerval revealed in moments of real insanity.

54. L. Aragon, *La Peinture au défi*, p. 8.
55. See great importance given to this subject between 1875-80, Charcot, *op. cit.*, p. 254.
56. Aragon, Breton, *op. cit.*, XI, 22.
57. L. Aragon, *Le Paysan de Paris*, p. 176.
58. J. M. Charcot, *op. cit.*, p. 158.
59. A. Breton, P. Eluard, *L'Immaculée Conception*, p. 30.

Expressing this simulation of mental disorder, however, involved, it was thought, a creative process whose first manifestation would be destructive. Along with reason, other human characteristics associated with logical thinking had to be banished. And first of all came *memory*—in so far as it is organized logical conservation of past experiences. Many are the expressions of disdain for the archives of memory. In his letter addressed to the "Voyantes," Breton finds himself "en haine de la mémoire, de cette combustion qu'elle entretient partout où je n'ai plus envie de rien voir"[60] and prefers to memory the chaotic, instinctive revelations of the Mediums. Crevel, speaking of the "soi-disants [*sic*] poètes," criticizes them for being "accrochés au souvenir, aux faits."[61] Desnos, in his *Confession d'un enfant du siècle*, asks himself if, as a matter of fact, he has any memories at all: "Ai-je des souvenirs au fait. Je suis arrivé à la perception de l'éternité. A quoi bon cataloguer faits matériels, car le rêve est aussi matériel que ces actions tangibles, ou aussi peu."[62] Hugnet glorifies the art of forgetting when he speaks of: ". . . Un explorateur envoyé par son pays pour étudier ici un art qui s'est perdu: l'art de l'oubli. Des prêtres, d'un culte inconnu, réunis au collège, massaient le crâne de celui qui voulait oublier. Du doigt, ils détruisaient sa mémoire."[63]

Memory has been replaced by "les souvenirs du présent"[64] and the unpredictability of the future, which would be governed by the mystical power of hazard; "le souvenir du futur"[65] as Breton calls it. In a selection, entitled "Il y aura une fois," he longs for the cultivation of this new memory: "Si . . . cet homme se risquait à arracher sa proie de mystère au passé? . . . S'il était, lui, vraiment résolu à n'ouvrir la bouche que pour dire: "Il y aura une fois. . . ."[66]

Another element to be discarded is the deep-rooted emotion of love for country and home; this evidence of man's stability, hu-

60. A. Breton, "Lettre aux Voyantes," *Révolution Surréaliste*, V, 22. See also "La Porte Albinos."

61. R. Crevel, *L'Esprit contre la raison*, p. 55.

62. Desnos. *Confession d'un enfant du siècle*, *Révolution Surréaliste*, VI, 19-20.

63. G. Hugnet, "Histoire d'Antoinette-la-Parricide," *Petite Anthologie poétique du Surréalisme*, p. 99.

64. P. Soupault, "Wang-Wang," *Anthologie de la nouvelle poésie française*, p. 434.

65. A. Breton, frontpiece to *Introduction au discours sur le peu de réalité*.

66. A. Breton, "Il y aura une fois," *Le Surréalisme au Service de la Révolution*, I, 4.

manity and love of order, was defied by the anti-social attitude of Breton and his contemporaries:

> Que d'autres s'attachent à leur famille, à leur pays et à la terre même, je ne connais pas cette sorte d'émulation. Je n'ai jamais aimé dans mon être que ce qu'il me paraissait y avoir en lui avec le dehors litigieux, de grandement contrastant.[67]

It will be seen in later chapters how the Romantic cult of sentiment gradually gave way to the cult of disorganized, ineffable instinct, and love of humanity to these anti-social leanings.

Finally, there must be destruction of logical language, which proves inadequate to express alienation of sensations, the "élans" of instinct, the "souvenirs du futur," which in short is incapable of conveying the desired mystical disorder. This aspect of Surrealism is the most obvious, of course, and the most strikingly unusual; and it has, therefore, often been mistaken for an end in itself, or a pose; it is rather a means of avoiding natural, orderly imagery in poetry by those who are seeking to create a new idiom to express the new poetic mysticism that they have conceived. From Mallarmé to Breton the poet will prefer silence to the risk of misrepresenting his newly found surreality. As Breton explains:

> Qu'est-ce qui me retient de brouiller l'ordre des mots, d'attenter de cette manière à l'existence toute apparente des choses! Le langage peut et doit être arraché à son servage. Plus de descriptions d'après nature, plus d'études de moeurs. Silence, afin qu'où nul n'a amais passé je passe, silence![68]

In his preface to the *Alphabet sourd aveugle* of Mesens, Paul Eluard scorns even the value attached to the symbols of language:

> Arrêtons-nous avant d'assembler les lettres. Au delà du possible, oublions la lecture, l'écriture, l'orthographe—et même la sensationnelle épellation des bègues.
>
> La lettre mange le mot comme une ligne droite infinie le dessin. Pure abstraction en soi, elle n'est vraiment concrète et objective que pour ces idiots qui en ont la perception brute.

---

67. A. Breton, "L'Etrange Diversion," *Introduction au discours sur le peu de réalité*, pp. 38-9.
68. *Ibid.*, p. 29.

C'est en considérant cette cécité psychique que Mesens nomme son alphabet: sourd aveugle.[69]

All these destructive reactions are not essential values but merely symptoms in the evolution of the mystical concept which drove the poet to the worship of disorder. It is these symptoms that will serve as guides in the tracing of the history of this development.

Beyond these symptoms will be seen the process of building up new positive values that might give to poetry and art the new formula sought by Aragon and his contemporaries: to create images and objects which in all their concrete character might give the human mind a representation of the infinite or the eternal without relegating the vision to another world. If reality, which is to be destroyed, is the apparent absence of contradiction, then "le merveilleux, c'est la contradiction qui apparait dans le réel."[70] It is through a contradiction in language, expressing the disordinate in nature as perceived by the irrational qualities of mind, that the poet arrives at this *merveilleux*, which has its roots in what used to be called the *absurd*. It is upon these premises that Nadja becomes a *real* person, although there is no question of her becoming "natural."[71] But she exists, gracefully hiding her face behind the heavy, nonexistent feather of her hat,[72] and sees a blue wind passing in the trees.[73] Time has acquired a new flexibility for those who view life thus:

> *Les rideaux qui n'ont jamais été levés*
> *Flottent aux fenêtres des maisons qu'on construira.*[74]

Space has been endowed with a wider scope:

> *Regarde-moi:*
> *La perspective ne joue pas pour moi*
> *Je tiens ma place*
> *Et tu ne peux pas t'en éloigner*
> *Il n'y a rien autour de moi*
> *Et, si je me détourne, rien est à deux faces:*
> *Rien et moi.*[75]

69. Preface of Eluard to Mesens' *Alphabet sourd aveugle.*
70. L. Aragon, *Le Paysan de Paris*, p. 251.
71. Breton, *Nadja*, p. 175.
72. *Ibid.*, p. 146.
73. *Ibid.*, p. 108.
74. Breton, "Textes Surréalistes," *Révolution Surréaliste*, VI, 6.
75. Eluard, *Défense de savoir*, p. 31.

According to the law of contradiction, the poet can make the laws of nature cease to exist; gravitation can disappear, fruits and flowers can don new colors, night change place with day, and the whole movement of existence pause in eternal expectancy. An artist like Eluard will indeed give the "Impossible Dawn" a terrible reality: "C'est par une nuit comme celle-ci que j'ai cueilli sur la verdure perpendiculaire des framboises blanches comme du lait."[76] In truth, he seems to have abolished both the visible, i.e. exterior reality, and the invisible, i.e. otherworldly mysticism. Between the visible and the invisible lies the eternal, according to this concept; they were not *blind,* those who could sense the infinite in the "miroir sans tain," and in all the other concrete entities on earth. One of the less read but most talented of the Surrealists gave this idea of the infinite perhaps its simplest and most concise form; in Francis Picabia's words: "Beaucoup de personnes cherchent à se représenter l'infini. Imaginez deux glaces ayant les mêmes formes et dimensions, posées en face l'une de l'autre: l'infini est le reflet qu'elles se renvoient."[77]

We must remember that empty yet teeming image of the infinite as we go back to the sources of the mystical atheism of which it is the fruit. As we trace its history we must watch for the more general, deeper characteristics underlying the aspects of Surrealism that persist today.

Behind the alienation of sensation lies the gradual growth of an anti-natural, anti-human, anti-social, anti-rational, anti-emotional attitude.

The explanation of the objective "hazard" is the ultimate result of the development of the illogical and the absurd as a substitute for the religious concept of the *merveilleux.*

"The great modern tradition" originating with Baudelaire will be made possible only because three generations of artists and poets will adhere to the principle of creative power through destruction.

In pointing out these elements we must determine how this new concept of mysticism has gradually transfigured traditional poetic themes.

76. Eluard, *Les Dessous d'une vie ou la Pyramide humaine,* p. 41.
77. Francis Picabia, "Pensées et Souvenirs," *Littérature,* Nouvelle Série, **IV,** 13.

CHAPTER II

The Romantic Background

I

BEFORE ROMANTICISM the French poetic ideal had been to paint human nature; in Boileau's well known words: "'Jamais de la nature il ne faut s'écarter." The unbelievable, the unrealistic were barred because they would leave the reader unmoved. The poet had to clarify his poetic visions so that the reader might share them with him. In this process it was imperative to maintain the natural hierarchy of things, to lay an emphasis on the broad, dominant contours of nature and to relegate details to their accepted subordination.

Although with the coming of Romanticism there was a shift in emphasis from the *reasonable* to the *emotional,* the poetic aim remained basically the same: more than ever there was revealed a love of humanity. Even physical nature was often invested with the attributes of human nature: for its main role in romantic poetry was to be the keeper of memories of human emotions, to which man clung even when they were no more. Love of both nature and man was manifested even in the attitude of the Romanticists toward death: when they sought death it was to perpetuate in eternal life what was most cherished in human life. It is true that at the same time there arose a weariness of the world, a revolt against the monotony of experiences that had become too well known; it was in truth a Romanticist, Alfred de Musset, who said: "Je suis venu trop tard dans un monde trop vieux." But how did the Romanticists seek to escape from the known to the unknown: through physical action, through concrete phenomena, such as a beautiful new landscape, a beautiful unknown face, a newly discovered country; all these had to be made intelligible and, therefore, had to be clothed in a new aspect of the familiar forms of nature. Despite the romantic *élan,* early French Romanticism, on the whole, preserved, as Paul Hazard points out in his analysis of "Les Caractères nationaux du lyrisme français," the traditional qualities of order, clarity, moderation:

> L'âme française a gardé ses qualités traditionnelles: goût obstiné de la composition et de l'ordre, clarté, netteté; modération au moins relative; . . . raison toujours vigilante; conscience des problèmes moraux; habitude de s'adresser non pas à des êtres d'exception, mais à l'être moyen, à l'être universel.[1]

Although the general character of Romanticism was, particularly in France, in many respects rational and basically naturalistic, there has been a tendency in recent times to link certain aspects of it with the basic characteristics of French poetry after 1870. The Surrealists have often very generously, perhaps too generously, acknowledged their debt to the Romanticists, particularly to the German Romanticists. Only recently in an interview,[2] André Breton put first among the influences which he felt had been significant in his work that of Achim von Arnim. In 1937 L'Ame romantique et le Rêve of Albert Béguin showed the cult of the dream as the basis of Romanticism and found in it a renewal of poetic mysticism, leading through the occultism of Nerval and Hugo to modern poetry. However, M. Béguin does not attempt to show any direct influence or even indicate precisely the relationship which he notices between the German Romanticists and what he calls the "second Romanticists" of France. On the other hand, in the same year an inquiry conducted by the Cahiers du Sud tended to prove that the German Romanticists had had no direct influence on French poetry:

> Sauf pour quelques initiés, parmi lesquels figurent la plupart des signataires de ce numéro spécial, la pensée et le rythme parlés du romantisme allemand nous sont transmis à la façon dont une photographie en noir et blanc transmet un tableau de maître.[3]

This problem of Romantic influences is, then, the first to be considered in an inquiry into the literary sources of Surrealism. In view of the fundamental characteristics of the new mysticism analyzed in the previous chapter, can the search for surreality be said to have its roots consciously or unconsciously in the spiritual manifestations of Roman-

1. P. Hazard, in Quatre Etudes, pp. 84-5.
2. The interview was granted to me on January 2, 1942.
3. "Le Romantisme allemand," Cahiers du Sud, XVI, 106-7.

ticism, or is there a definite break and a complete renewal of poetic inspiration?

Mysticism is an essential characteristic of that large literary output of the nineteenth century which has been associated with the concept of "Romanticism." As historians of Romanticism have pointed out, the nineteenth century became greatly interested in occultism. Illuminism, which had had earlier enthusiasts in the last days of the "'Ancien Régime,"[4] had regained the attention of men of letters. Various forms of occultism were in vogue in France throughout the century: Swedenborgism, Mesmerism, and oriental occultism.

About 1830 it can be noticed that this increasing interest in illuminism is beginning to modify the earlier pantheism of the Romanticists. After his return from a voyage to the Near East, Lamartine writes in a letter to Virieu in December 1834: "la forme religieuse veut et crie révolution."[5] Both Lamartine and Balzac, and of course Nerval later on, find in the mysticism of the Orient a more complex process of ascension toward the infinite, than that of the Christian resurrection after death. What the Romantic visionaries took from oriental illuminism was primarily the idea of metempsychosis—a gradual transmutation from one form of life to another, a series of expiations leading to infinite existence. It is as if terrestrial existence moved along a road to the Absolute; the beginning of the road seems almost completely paved with material substance; gradually matter is mingled with spiritual essence, and as physical existence finds its way toward the infinite, the ratio between the material and the spiritual changes until matter at last completely disappears. Balzac's *Louis Lambert* (1832) and *Séraphita* (1833) are human beings that have progressed somewhat farther than most on this roadway. Lambert's apparent insanity and incoherence are evidences of a lucidity incomprehensible to the average man; for Louis Lambert is breathing heavenly air before his time, and, having lost much of his contact with the finite world, he can no longer communicate with those who surround him physically. In this instance, Balzac, like the Surrealists, tends to consider insanity as a manifestation of human contact with the infinite.

Victor Hugo was likewise acquainted with the various forms of occultism of his epoch. But it was not until the time of his exile that the

4. See Auguste Viatte, *Victor Hugo et les Illuminés de son temps*, pp. 113-4.
5. Quoted from Henri Guillemin, *Le Jocelyn de Lamartine*, p. 215.

pseudo altars of spiritualism and table-turning seances really played an important part in his life and directly influenced his literary work. Victor Hugo was already interested in Cabalism before he left France. In 1853 Mme. de Girardin brings from Paris to the exiles of Guernsey the vogue of the turning tables. In ecstatic poses Hugo listens to God and helps the tables speak. . . .[6] In his metaphysical poems *Ce que dit la bouche d'ombre* and *Dieu*, written between 1854 and 1855, he expresses the struggle of the mystic as he travels through various stages of comprehension and perception of the infinite. In *Dieu* we find Hugo first faced with the positivism of the average man, whom he interprets as saying:

> *Je m'oppose, homme, à l'excès de connaître*
> *De chercher, de trouver, d'errer, d'aller au bout;*[7]

and insisting that "nul ne doit sortir de son possible."[8] He proceeds to the poet, whose wish it is to:

> *Unir la terre au ciel, et dans le même nœud*
> *L'idéal au réel, et tisser une étoile.*[9]

He goes on to the Bat and the Owl who despair and doubt, in their incapacity to arrive "au delà du réel, au delà du possible,"[10] to the Crow who finds himself torn between the spirit and the senses, to the prophetic Eagle who feels that he has attained the vision, and the Griffon and Angel who tell man how to soar to this vision.

It is when taking the point of view of the Bat and the Angel that Hugo is most successful in conveying the impression of new visions, expressing, in terms of the Bat, man's handicap as he seeks the infinite; in terms of the Angel, his possible triumph over these limitations. He is among the first to establish a vocabulary suitable to the evocation of the unknown. "L'invisible erre dans l'impalpable"[11] might have come from the pen of Stephane Mallarmé. When he writes: "L'éternité tordant les minutes de l'heure!"[12] he is indeed trying here to sever the

6. See A. Viatte, *op. cit.*, and Paul Hazard, *Victor Hugo en exil.*
7. V. Hugo, *Œuvres inédites, Dieu*, p. 7.
8. *Ibid.*, p. 11.
9. *Ibid.*, p. 46.
10. *Ibid.*, p. 103.
11. *Ibid.*, p. 179.
12. *Ibid.*, p. 181.

infinite from the finite. And through the tortured Owl he dares to envisage something beyond human dreams:

> *Et parfois j'aperçois même, au delà du rêve*
> *Dans des fonds où mes yeux n'étaient jamais venus,*
> *Des levers effrayants de mondes inconnus:*[13]

Expressions like "Titan du relatif et nain de l'absolu"[14] or "L'homme est un désir vaste en une étreinte étroite"[15] express the feeling of human limitations. Moreover, attempting to surmount the poetic inadequacy of words, he sensed the effectiveness of negative terms in defining unknown quantities, a technique which was to be developed by later poets to a great extent:

> *Pas de droite et de gauche*
> *Pas de haut ni de bas; . . .*
> *Point de temps; point d'ici, point de là; point d'espace.*[16]

Yet can it be said that this cult of illuminism brought into the literary work of those who are considered to be essentially "Romanticists" a change of technique resulting from a transformation of attitude toward life and death? It appears to me that the occultism of the Romanticists is, on the whole, the end of one concept rather than the beginning of a new one.

The Romanticist's ideal of life, whether it be terrestrial or otherwise, is happiness. Most of his writing is a protest against the imperfection and frustration of happiness here on earth. Going back to the earliest Romanticists, we find Jean-Paul or Novalis trying to locate in the world of the invisible their Clothilde or Sophie who are lost to the visible world. Just as Albert Béguin points out in his analysis of the work of Jean-Paul, the leimotiv of this poetic mysticism is an "appel de la créature aimante vers une région où l'amour soit enfin parfait."[17] It can readily be seen that this region wherein perfection is invested with ultimate reality is for the German Romanticist synonymous with the Biblical paradise, toward which his tremendous and sincere religious propensity leads him. As a matter of fact, a number of Hoelderlin's poems

---

13. V. Hugo, *op. cit.*, p. 106.
14. *Ibid.*, p. 205.
15. *Ibid.*, p. 210.
16. *Ibid.*, p. 240.
17. A. Béguin, *L'Ame romantique et le Rêve*, II, 55.

were inspired by Biblical symbols. In the same way, Jean-Paul saw as
the limit of his many-sided dreams the symbols of Christianity, which
to him most adequately represented the supernatural. His dreams in
Hesperus are full of the presence of Christ and the Virgin. With
Novalis we find the dream becoming an even more direct gateway to
heaven:

> *Hinunter zu der süssen Braut*
> *Zu Jesus, dem Geliebten—*
> *Getrost, die Abenddämmrung graut*
> *Den Liebenden, Betrübten.*
> *Ein Traum bricht unsre Banden los*
> *Und senkt uns in des Vaters Schoss.*[18]

In the background of all his nocturnal visions in *Hymnen an die Nacht*
is the conviction that: "Unverbrennlich steht das Kreuz—eine Sieges-
fahne unsers Geschlechts."[19] Later, Victor Hugo's attitude is much the
same. The unknown to him is also synonymous with God who alone
can establish an equilibrium in the equation between what is evident
and what is incomprehensible to man. To arrive at an understanding
of God or the unknown he must comprehend the order with which
the universe has been endowed.[20]

In preparing to perceive the universal order it is essential for the
Romanticist to sense the ideal of harmony in his earthly surroundings.
Nature is the medium in his immediate possession for the expression of
this ideal harmony. In Jean-Paul's representation of paradise, in Novalis' concept of eternity, in Hugo's voyage toward the infinite, the
goal is the final evolution of man's aspiration for harmony and order.
In his hymn to the "Goddess of Harmony" early in the history of Romantic literature, Hoelderlin formulated this faith in the ultimate one-
ness and harmony of all love and all other human emotion:

> *Geister! Brüder! unser Bund erglühe*
> *Von der Liebe göttlicher Magie,*
> *Unbegrenzte, reine Liebe ziehe*
> *Freundlich uns zur hohen·Harmonie.*[21]

18. Novalis, *Schriften*, I, 66.
19. *Ibid.*, p. 59.
20. See *Dieu*, pp. 235-6.
21. Hoelderlin, *Gesammelte Dichtungen*, I, 108.

Hence nature and reality have but a relative meaning and cannot constitute a medium for the search of the absolute. If there is disorder and imperfection, then poetry that is inspired by mysticism should tend to transcend this disorder and certainly not make of it a cult. In this transcendentalism lies of course the basis of the Romantic philosophy of nature which, as E. Spenlé so keenly observed, interprets the inferior by the superior forms of existence:

> . . . Il verra dans ce qui est 'en bas' l'ébauche de ce qui est 'en haut'; il surprendra ce 'nisus' sacré qui soulève le monde dans toutes ses parties, qui porte la pierre vers la plante, la plante vers l'animal, l'animal vers l'homme, et l'homme vers Dieu. . . . La connaissance de la nature sera donc nécessairement religieuse et symboliste.[22]

Nor did an increasing interest in illuminism, it seems to me, drastically change Romantic values. It is true that the poet saw himself more and more as a visionary and felt himself increasingly at home among the occult forces of the universe. But the dominant element which unites all the Romanticists, whether they be profoundly Christian or inspired by some other form of mysticism, is their ideal of progress and ultimate perfection. Any concept of the infinite is irrevocably tied up with the idea of progress. Herbert J. Hunt emphasizes this aspect of Romanticism in his book on *The Epic in Nineteenth Century France*:

> It was a mania among nineteenth century poets to make of progress not merely a law of nature, but a fundamental religious dogma, satisfying of itself and capable of unifying all men and electrifying them to beneficial action.[23]

Hugo himself stated this clearly: "Toute étude sérieuse sur l'infini conclut au progrès. La perfection contemplée démontre la perfectibilité."[24] The illuminist concept of metempsychosis serves as an excellent means of representing in art the ascension of man toward this perfection.[25] The later mysticism, on the contrary, will interpret the superior by the

22. E. Spenlé, *Novalis*, p. 191.
23. Herbert J. Hunt, *The Epic in Nineteenth Century France*, p. 405.
24. Note pour *Les Misérables* (ed. Ollendorff, 1862), p. 311 (quoted from A. Viatte, *op. cit.*).
25. See for example Lamartine's *La Chute d'un ange*.

inferior forms of existence, and, ipso facto, reduce the order to disorder, which in turn will represent the unknown and the absolute.

As a matter of fact, one may well ask if the unconditional acceptance of natural law and ultimate harmony is compatible with
the search for surreality here on earth. Romantic dreams of the
supernatural, inspired as they were by religious faith in an afterlife,
held in abeyance the realization of the dream. If out of the dissatisfaction that the Surrealist experienced with the physical world
about him arose impatience and a desire to destroy what caused his
dissatisfaction, the mysticism of the Romanticist, on the other hand,
was accompanied by a *severing* of relations with that which caused him
dissatisfaction; instead of trying to *change* reality, the Romanticist
pointed his interest elsewhere:

> *Was sollen wir auf dieser Welt*
> *Mit unsrer Lieb' und Treue*
> *Das Alte wird hintangestellt,*
> *Was soll uns dann das Neue.*[26]

"Sehnsucht nach dem Tod" is the title of this poem of Novalis.
Death looms all important in the poetry of those who seek the unknown without wishing to deviate from nature. The Romanticist
indeed serves in the temple of heavenly death.[27] For him death is
the only realm where the sublime can be experienced.[28] It is death
which, according to Hoelderlin,

> *Führt aus Hüllen der Nacht hinüber*
> *In der Erkenntnisse Land.*[29]

Among the French Romanticists the same attitude toward death was
prevalent from the very beginning. Chateaubriand expresses it in
René: "Homme, la saison de ta migration n'est pas encore venue; at-
tends que le vent de la mort se lève, alors tu déploieras ton vol vers ces
régions inconnues que ton cœur demande."

Various symbols had been introduced to name the invisible and
indicate the impossibility of attaining the vision here on earth. They
became public property: Novalis' blue flower, Alterbom's isle of

26. Novalis, *op. cit.,* p. 65.
27. *Ibid.,* p. 65.
28. Hoelderlin, *op. cit.,* "Der Rhein," p. 268.
29. *Ibid.,* "Der Tod," p. 281.

bliss. Typical is a dream passage in George Sand's *Lettres d'un Voyageur*. After relating numerous real voyages, Sand ventures to describe a landscape reached in the inactivity of dreams. It is supposed to represent an unknown land to which she is beckoned by "des âmes inconnues"[30] which have not known life on this earth. The locale is visualized as an island: "elle doit exister sur la terre, ou dans quelqu'une de ces planètes."[31] It is a virgin land where blue roses grow, and which can be peopled at will "d'affections saintes et de bonheur impossible."[32] But all that remains of these strange dreams is just enough to make the author sense the impotence of human imagination and memory. If one could but retain the speech and physical aspects of this "rêve quasi-mystique,"[33] Sand thinks that it would perhaps be possible to write "le poème le plus fantastique que le siècle ait encore produit."[34]

Despite his many metaphysical speculations, Hugo held the same conviction: humanity can sense the absolute but will fail to represent it adequately:

> *Nulle forme ne vit loin du réel traînée;*
> *La vision terrestre à la terre est bornée.*[35]

The barriers of the material world will disappear in good time. According to Hugo, were the visionary to try to penetrate the mysteries too soon, nature, that faithful dog of man, would stop in terror at the threshold of the abyss.[36] And Hugo, like most of the Romanticists, had too great a love of nature and its order to revolt against its laws.[37] Although at the time that he was writing *Dieu*, he took part in spiritual seances, he refused to mingle the revelations

---

30. G. Sand, *Lettres d'un voyageur*, p. 34.
31. *Ibid.*, p. 34.
32. *Ibid.*, p. 38.
33. *Ibid.*, p. 34.
34. *Ibid.*, p. 35.
35. Hugo, "Le Calcul c'est l'abîme," *Toute la lyre*, I, 274.
36. *Ibid.*, p. 274.
37. Only rarely does Hugo attempt distortions of nature such as the following passage in which he wants to give an idea of what the visionary might experience:

> Nous entendons le bruit du rayon que Dieu lance,
> La voix de ce que l'homme appelle le silence.
>
> —*Contemplations*, p. 427.

of the turning tables with his consciously written poetry.[38] He felt
that the verses that came out of these seances should be barred from
the *reasonable* works of the poet. He felt loath to plunge too deep
into the forbidden mysteries and had a great contempt for the
"savant" as opposed to the "voyant." The "savant," according to
Hugo, erroneously believes that by attempting to clarify the unknown and
to reduce it to the limits of his scientific knowledge, he will find the ultimate reality and truth.

> O science! absolu qui proscrit l'inouï!
> L'exact pris pour le vrai! la plus grande méprise
> De l'homme.[39]

Man, he explains, despite all his efforts, knows nothing of the
greater reality; he alone is a visionary who will wait for death: it
is the only solution to his avid desire, and Hugo has expressed this
thought beautifully in his final verses of *Dieu*:

> Veux-tu, flèche tremblante, atteindre enfin ta cible?
> Veux-tu toucher le but, regarder l'invisible;
> L'innommé, l'idéal, le réel, l'inouï?
> Comprendre, déchiffrer, lire? être un ébloui?
> Veux-tu planer plus haut que la sombre nature?
> Veux-tu dans la lumière inconcevable et pure
> Ouvrir tes yeux, par l'ombre affreuse appesantis?
> Le veux-tu? Réponds.
> —Oui! criai-je
> Et je sentis
> Que la création tremblait comme une toile
> Il me toucha le front du doigt
> Et je mourus.[40]

As Hugo grew older this attitude became even more pronounced.
Although he was attuned to the existence of "autres choses" he

38. See *Journal de l'exil*, cited by Berret in *La Philosophie de V. Hugo* (1854-9).

39. Hugo, *Toute la Lyre*, I, 277.

40. Hugo, *Dieu*, p. 262-3. For same idea see also: "Les Quatre Vents de l'esprit," p. 93 and p. 150.

asked: "Pourquoi sonder l'abîme? Attendons."[41] and forced himself to wait:

> O mon âme, en cherchant l'azur ton vol dévie.......
> Revenons à la terre
> Pour retourner au ciel.[42]

Hugo was old, and he could wait. But those who were calling themselves visionaries even as he was saying "revenons à la terre" and resigning himself to his earthly prison, were like his "Hibou" rather than his "Ange," ready to use their claws in order to: "ôter, enfin, la nuit du visage inconnu."[43] Inspired neither by love of humanity nor of nature, their attempt to seize the unknown had little relation to the Romanticists' ascension to God. In their case it was to be a question of "plonger" rather than "monter."

From the earliest German to the last French manifestations, the Romantic dream of the infinite had been based on nature's hierarchies, motivated by a search for happiness, inspired by a belief in perfectibility. It is these very pillars of Romanticism that will be disdained and deemed obstacles to poetic creation and artistic freedom. With the Romantic dream the later French poetic visions have but one affinity: a passion for the unknown. But the cause, the direction and above all the expression will prove of an entirely different metal.

II

While most of the Romanticists relegated the invisible and the supernatural to an existence beyond death, there were others who already were attempting to express through their human perceptions what they believed to lie outside of nature's framework.

The most important of these are Achim von Arnim and Gérard de Nerval. The German writer's interpretations of legendary material, and Nerval's *Aurélia, Les Filles du feu,* and *Le Voyage en Orient* cannot technically be included in the field of poetry; but

41. Hugo, *Œuvres complètes, Poésies XVI,* "Les Quatre Vents de l'esprit," p. 93.
42. *Ibid.,* pp. 149-50.
43. Hugo, *Dieu,* p. 116.

since the Surrealist poets, the origin of whose poetic inspiration we are attempting to analyze, give major importance to these two writers who fall chronologically within the period called Romantic, it is well to evaluate their contribution in the development of the new poetic mysticism.

As noted previously, the Surrealists believed that the supernatural character of legendary material and illogical phenomena in dreams could be effectively utilized as the expression of the surreal, of the plane of existence lying between the visible and the invisible. Many of them have indicated that the first definite examples of this tendency were to be seen in the tales of Achim von Arnim, a group of which had been translated into French in 1856 as *Contes bizarres* by Théophile Gautier fils, and in many of the writings of Nerval. Stories such as "Isabella von Aegypten" and "Die Majorats-Herren" are neither legend nor reality. In them legendary beliefs and superstitions are incorporated into a narrative which constantly keeps in touch with reality. As André Breton explains in his preface to the 1933 edition of *Contes bizarres*, Arnim's secret is: ". . . De douer d'une vie des plus acceptables certaines figures inanimées, aussi aisément qu'il parvient à priver graduellement de vie des créatures dans lesquelles nous avions tout lieu de croire que le sang circulait."[44] Thus, the "mandragore" and the golem in "Isabella," and the characters that people the visions produced by the mental disorder of the Majorats-Herr take on concrete forms, while Bella and Esther and the Majorats-Herr himself, dominated as they are by the disorder with which their existence is forever in contact, seem to incorporate elements of it within their own being.

"Isabella," based on the real historical figures of Isabelle of Egypt and Charles V of Spain, begins with the substitution of the real for the phantom. Bella is thought to be a ghost when she enters into what he believes to be a haunted abode. When Charles falls in love with her as a spectre, it is up to Bella to make him love the concrete form of the phantom. With this ultimate end in mind she gives life to legendary beings until they are undistinguishable from the real characters of the tale: the result is a company composed of a sorcerer, a golem replica of Bella, a dead man acting as if alive, and a young man created out of the stump of a tree.

In "Die Majorats-Herren" we find a much more developed tech-

44. A. von Arnim, *Contes bizarres*, p. 15.

nique: here, there is not only a mingling of real and legendary characters, but a juxtaposition of real and dream action in the composition of the intrigue. The hero's arrival, his acquaintance with his surroundings, and the visions which he experiences through his own eyes and those of his beautiful neighbor, Esther, are completely interrelated and interdependent. For instance, the weird revelation he has concerning his identity, through an hallucination, turns out, by the workings of chance, to coincide with the truth.

This same structure is evident in *Aurélia* and in parts of *Voyage en Orient* and *Les Filles du feu* of Gérard de Nerval. In *Aurélia*, the dreams that Nerval has of his beloved are intermingled with an account of his concrete daily existence, which is intermittently tormented by attacks of insanity. Beginning with a candid explanation of the author's illness, the narrative in *Aurélia* is for a time based on actual experience. Gérard de Nerval gives details of thoroughly acceptable circumstances of life, speaks once or twice of nocturnal dreams and strange visions in his sleep. But suddenly there begins an adventure of a different nature. He is walking on a real street with a real friend but with premonitions of revelations to come. Suddenly his friend leaves him, and it is as if the symbol of reality were departing and thrusting him, without his realizing it, into a world of illusion. The transition between the previous state and the present one is carried out in almost logical sequence. After the friend leaves, Gérard de Nerval continues on his way; but he is now going toward a star; and when he remarks: "je quittais mes habits terrestres et je les dispersais autour de moi,"[45] the hallucination is presented on the same plane of reality as the previous departure of his friend.

Earlier examples of the intermingling of two planes of vision occur in parts of *Voyage en Orient* and *Les Filles du feu*. For instance, in the part of the *Voyage en Orient* entitled "Druses et Maronites," Nerval tells us the story of an old and a new hashish eater. Under the influence of the drug, Yousouf, the addict, tells Hakem, the neophyte, what he considers to be an unbelievable tale. It is an account of a hashish vision. It begins as the familiar dream which Yousouf always has under the effect of the drug: while he is moving along the Nile, the celestial figure of a woman appears out of the heart of the infinite. There is nothing strange so far, as it is un-

45. G. de Nerval, *Aurélia*, p. 16.

mistakably a dream and an ordinary experience for the addict. But since the potion on this particular night is weaker than usual, Yousouf has suddenly the impression of awaking within the framework of his dream and of finding the imaginary figure transformed into a living person. The experience which began as an illusion seems to end as a reality. In the morning the illusion and the reality have become so perfectly fused in his memory that he can no longer be sure whether he is in love with a fairy or a real person. Yousouf concludes that the effect of hashish on the mind lies not so much in the drug's power to create illusions as to confuse reality with the dream: "J'arrive à croire parfois que tout cela n'était qu'une illusion de cette herbe perfide, qui attaque ma raison peut-être . . . si bien que je ne sais plus déjà même distinguer ce qui est rêve de ce qui est réalité.[46]

In *Les Filles du feu* this same blending of fantasy with reality occurs through the interweaving of folklore material and actual events. Particularly in "Pandora," which really belongs apart and represents the most complete mental disorder of the author, there is no indication at all of any transition between reality and illusion. Having written a letter to Pandora, the author retires for the night but is unable to sleep. Whereupon begins a vision which gradually evolves into the absurdities of a nightmare. Since the preceding incidents had not put the reader in a state of receptivity for the absurd, the avalanche of events falls completely beyond the range of reason. Finally when all sense of time and place is lost, Nerval suddenly resorts to reality, exclaiming: "Je me jetai hors du lit comme un fou."[47]

Thus, Nerval was bringing into his literary work a new plane of logic by which, he thought, might be told a new history of the world "mêlée de souvenirs d'études et de fragments de songes,"[48] the logic of the insane, of which we have seen an earlier example in Arnim's *Die Majorats-Herren*. The acceptance of the real and the dream on the same basis affects the concept of time and place, which are in turn shrunk or expanded; in *Aurélia*, we find Nerval explaining:

Pour moi, déjà, le temps de chaque jour semblait augmenté de

46. Nerval, *Voyage en Orient*, II, 344.
47. Nerval, *Les Filles du feu*, p. 319.
48. Nerval, *Aurélia*, p. 39.

deux heures; de sorte qu'en me levant aux heures fixées par les horloges de la maison, je ne faisais que me promener dans l'empire des ombres. Les compagnons qui m'entouraient me semblaient endormis et pareils aux spectres de Tarbare, jusqu'à l'heure où pour moi se levait le soleil. Alors je saluais cet astre par une prière, et ma vie réelle commençait.[49]

This distorting of the time element produces certain images in which the dead and the living are intermingled, as in Arnim's tales, and exist simultaneously on the same plane of reality. In one of his hallucinations, for example, Nerval sees a clock and on the clock a bird that speaks of his family dead *or* living: "L'oiseau me parlait de personnes de ma famille vivantes ou mortes en divers temps, comme si elles existaient simultanément."[50] And elsewhere in *Aurélia:* "Je distinguai quelques personnes qui m'étaient connues, les unes vivantes, d'autres mortes en divers temps."[51] This association of the dead with the living will become an important element of the later poetic mysticism.

The origin of this tendency to distort time can be found in *Les Filles du feu* where Nerval often speaks simultaneously of events that are not related except in the subconscious life of the author. Most of the tales included in *Les Filles du feu* depend for their narration on this freedom from the notion of time. "Sylvie" might have been an ordinary love story deeply steeped in reality, had it been recounted in the accepted sequence of events or totally in retrospect. But Nerval was to express his power to "voir se presser en quelques minutes les tableaux les plus saillants d'une longue période de la vie."[52] During a ride at four in the morning between Paris and Loisy are crowded all the incidents of the past just as one would recall them in a state of drowsiness; interpolated between them are the dreams of the past, which become identified with reality. It is with a shock that we waver from the past to the present, from the real to the unreal, from the visible to the invisible as the narrative flows on. The same procedure is also used in "Octavie" and "Pandora," both of which with logical transitions might have become quite acceptable to reason. In these tales, in the short space between two

49. *Ibid.,* p. 96.
50. *Ibid.,* p. 21.
51. *Ibid.,* p. 56.
52. Nerval, *Les Filles du feu,* p. 178.

encounters are interpolated events which are controlled by an abnormal time and place concept; the result is that instead of giving the reader a harmonious unity of impression, the author leaves us the disorder of detached images, rising out of spontaneous, chance memories rather than directed ones.

Another of Nerval's illusions in *Aurélia* which will later be utilized is that of finding one's self exteriorized and forming part of the new perspective. It is with fright that Nerval appears before his own eyes, distorted by his hallucination: "O terreur! ô colère! c'était mon visage, c'était toute ma forme idéalisée et grandie."[53] It is an impression that Baudelaire and later Alfred Jarry have in their experience with hashish. This type of exteriorization will contribute considerably to the general distortion of perspective which will be attempted by the seekers of surreality.

Toward the end of *Aurélia,* Gerard de Nerval reveals a marked crescendo in his hallucinations as the moments of insanity become more grave and more prolonged. As his control over his perceptions is gradually weakened, real sensations mingle more and more with his illusions. Walking in front of the Louvre, he suddenly seems to be witnessing the end of the world: "Arrivé vers le Louvre, je marchai jusqu'à la place, et là, un spectacle étrange m'attendait. A travers des nuages rapidement chassés par le vent, je vis plusieurs lunes qui passaient avec une grande rapidité."[54]

Gradually we find Nerval's hallucinations leading him into the occult realm of nature. Though he feels himself a captive on earth, he has the impression at moments of actually freeing himself of his physical limitations; magnetic rays emanating from him and from other forms of existence seem to link him to a universal network and to make it possible for him to sense harmonies heretofore unimagined.[55]

But it is Nerval's explanation of his state of mind, rather than his description of visions that are neither completely real nor imaginary, that throws light upon the poetry to come:

> La seule différence pour moi de la veille au sommeil était que, dans la première, tout se transfigurait à mes yeux; chaque personne qui m'approchait semblait changée, les objets matériels avaient comme

53. Nerval, *Aurélia,* p. 49.
54. *Ibid.,* p. 85.
55. *Ibid.,* p. 97.

une pénombre qui en modifiait la forme, et les yeux de la lumière, les combinaisons des couleurs se décomposaient, de manière à m'entretenir dans une série constante d'impressions qui se liaient entre elles, et dont le rêve, plus dégagé des éléments extérieurs, continuait la probabilité.[56]

The type of world indicated in these lines, a world where the real and the concrete are taken as a basis and then distintegrated and illuminated, is what Rimbaud and those who follow in his footsteps will seek to express in poetry.

Even as Balzac's *Louis Lambert*, *Aurélia* had pointed to the relativity of the concept of sanity. Because of his mental aberrations Nerval found himself controlled by forces much more potent than those understood by human reason.

Thus, it may be said that Arnim and Nerval, more than most of the other writers of the Romantic period, had opened the way to a new representation of the supernatural. In their works can be seen the intermingling of the spiritual and the physical, with a basis in the logic of insanity. But does this imply a mysticism that denies harmony in art and in life, and which consciously seeks the disorder of the universe as a gateway toward a greater reality? Is there in these works disdain of humanity, a will to destroy the natural framework that constitutes exterior reality?

In his introduction to his translation of Arnim, Théophile Gautier fils admires Arnim for not having the French mania for explaining everything, even including what is supposed to be fantastic.[57] But is this really true? Is the mingling of two spheres of concepts accepted as a goal? Are we really dealing here with an attempt at an aberration of the mental faculty that creates the work of art, as is true in later French poetic works? Examination of *Die Majorats-Herren* in detail shows that every phenomenon that overflows into fantasy has its reverse side dipped into nature, every incident that beckons to the deepest recesses of the illogical has another face that makes it acceptable to reason. No sooner has the Majorats-Herr appeared than he has a vision of phantoms; his very sane cousin immediately explains that he is seeing a Jewish ritual,

56. Nerval, *Aurélia*, p. 19.
57. T. Gautier fils, *Introduction* to tr. *Contes bizarres, Arnim*, p. 28.

bizarre but actually taking place. Later he perceives a weird crow, which he takes for a supernatural omen of bad tidings; we find it is nothing more than a black bonnet. He hears the flapping of the wings of the angel of death; but Esther realizes that it is a draught and closes the door violently. He sees mystical doves flying in the night; they are his cousin's pigeons disturbed in their sleep. After Esther's death, the Majorats-Herr has a Biblical vision of Adam and Eve; it is only a painting suspended above the door of her chamber. The Majorats-Herr dies for having drunk, according to Jewish superstition, from the water in the room where death had entered; but early in the story the Majorats-Herr had told us that because of his ill health he would not be able to live through the change of season that was taking place, and that we were to expect his death at any moment.

But what of the intermingling of supernatural and natural phenomena to a point where it becomes impossible to distinguish the one from the other? The dream or vision is not as mingled with exterior reality as one is apt to think at a first reading. By a clever literary trick the author indicates to the reader exactly when the natural is to end and the supernatural to begin, and he thus avoids the disorder that later writers will purposely seek. Esther is the medium through whose disequilibrium the Majorats-Herr can experience fantastic visions. This disorder was caused, as the author explains, by shock due to the sudden death of Esther's fiancé in a duel; thence, every vision of the supernatural is preceded by the hearing of a gun shot by the Majorats-Herr. It is as if parentheses were being put around the supernatural and a temporary pause being created in the narrative. It is only in the very last scene that the real action and the dream are simultaneous, and that the Majorats-Herr, calmly witnessing what he believes to be a visionary representation of the death of Esther, realizes that "dans tout ce qu'il avait vu, il y avait quelque chose qui s'était passé véritablement dans le monde ordinaire."[58] And yet André Breton claims Arnim as his first and foremost predecessor in his preface to the 1933 edition of Gautier's translation. In emphasizing the intermingling of the real and the unreal he cites Arnim as saying:

"Je discerne avec peine ce que je vois avec les yeux de la réalité de ce que voit mon imagination."[59]

58. Arnim, *Contes bizarres*, p. 195.
59. *Ibid.*, p. 171.

The original text shows that what Arnim emphasized was the exact opposite:

"Ich kann *genau* unterscheiden was ich mit dem Auge der Wahrheit sehen muss oder was ich mir gestalte."[60]

He can *exactly* distinguish the difference and sees to it that his reader does the same; the basis of his representation of the unusual is not a voluntary disorder of the mental process. It would appear that André Breton faithfully adhered to the mistranslation of Gautier, which made Arnim's text much more interesting from the point of view of Surrealism than the original. Had he consulted Arnim instead of trusting Gautier for his citation he would undoubtedly have lost a good argument—and perhaps an ancestor!

According to Gautier, Arnim would tell us that: "à travers le système de notre monde il apparut un monde supérieur que la fantaisie seule rend visible à l'esprit."[61] But "Sinnen," the word used in the original, cannot be translated as "esprit;"[62] Arnim was talking of the senses and not of the mind. He was not contemplating a revolution in the mental process as a means of creating a new art, but only a new adjustment of the senses in the manner of another Romanticist, William Blake, who said in his *Marriage of Heaven and Hell*: "If the doors of perception were cleansed, everything would appear to man as it is, infinite. For man has closed himself up till he sees all things through narrow chinks of his cavern." Arnim believed in the hierarchy of nature and in the divine power of God, which regulated it. Toward the end of "Isabella" he asked: "Mais qui donc remue notre cerveau? n'est-ce pas celui qui fait mouvoir toujours également et selon des changements réguliers les étoiles à la voûte du ciel?"[63]

In the case of *Aurélia*, is the disorder, created by the mingling of the real and the supernatural, the artistic motive of Gérard de Nerval to a greater extent than in the case of Arnim? On the contrary! When Nerval wrote on a confessional note the tragic account of visions induced by his intermittent insanity, his pathological experience, to which he gave successful artistic form in his quasi-lucid moments, was not an active revolt against nature but an attempt to give logical interpretation

60. Arnim, *Werke*, II, *Novellen*, p. 208, (the underlining is mine).
61. Arnim, *Contes bizarres*, p. 195.
62. Many are the inaccuracies caused by the substitution of the abstract for the concrete.
63. Arnim, *op. cit.*, p. 125.

to his abnormal perceptions. As Georges Dumas has pointed out in his study of insanity in *Les Etats intellectuels dans la mélancolie,* the dominant mental characteristic of the deranged is an attempt at conformity with natural laws rather than an exploitation of the disorder they unwittingly experience: "C'est la pensée qui continue son œuvre de coördination en dépit de toutes les incohérences, c'est l'esprit qui ne peut se résoudre à l'absurde et qui raisonne, qui interprète, qui systématise."[64]

Rarely does Nerval sacrifice to his mental aberration his literary equilibrium and artistic coherence. The intention of the strange tale of *Aurélia* is not to mystify or to revolutionize literary technique. Already in *Voyage en Orient,* when he was trying to convey an impression of the effects of hashish, Nerval had expressed the hallucinations by vague expressions such as: "une exaltation extraordinaire" or "des essaims de pensées nouvelles, inouïes, inconcevables, traversaient son âme en tourbillons de feu."[65] It was his belief that human language could only express sensations which conformed with our nature.[66] The extraordinary could be asserted but not expressed. In *Aurélia,* therefore, although the artist's soul is attuned to mysteries beyond the scope of the normal mind, he tries to give these revelations a lucid artistic transcription by utilizing as much as possible the known forms of chimera and metaphysical speculation.

Nerval candidly admits—and it is a recurring theme in *Aurélia*—that he has crises of insanity and that at such times it has seemed to him almost possible to establish contact with the hereafter and with his beloved Aurélia, recently lost. There are two separate worlds in *Aurélia,* as in Arnim's tales; the world of fantasy and dream, and the world of the artist who is forever trying to put order in his visions and to explain them to his reader, whom he has taken into his confidence. From the beginning Gérard de Nerval draws a line between his normal life and his hallucination. He reiterates: "Cette nuit-là, je fis un rêve,"[67] a pathetic refrain that represents his constant effort to sever his hallucinations from the rest of his life experiences.

Aurélia represents a world created by an abnormal mind, and recognized as such by its author. While later poets were to simulate this world and introduce it into the realm of the sane, Gérard de Nerval

64. G. Dumas, *Les Etats intellectuels dans la mélancolie,* p. 67.
65. Nerval, *Voyage en Orient,* II, 316.
66. *Ibid.,* p. 345.
67. Nerval, *Aurélia,* p. 11.

terms it "l'épanchement du songe dans la vie réelle" and calls it the illusion of a sick mind rather than the revelation of a greater reality. As Henri Clouard very aptly points out: "Revenue de ses visions dès le lendemain des crises, réveillé de ses rêves, Gérard de Nerval a reconnu et déclaré l'illusion. Quand il interprète le rêve comme une communication avec l'au-delà et le monde des esprits, il sait que c'est hypothèse."[68] Nerval's recognition of it as an hypothesis reveals an attitude entirely contrary to that of the poets of a later generation. Although, as we have seen, he often senses the intermingling of the earthly with the supernatural in his hallucinations, he finds himself unable to represent this relationship: "C'est un de ces rapports étranges dont je ne me rends pas compte moi-même et qu'il est plus aisé d'indiquer que de définir."[69]

His visions, therefore—as translated into literary form—follow for the most part the mysticism of the Bible, the idealism of the Utopists, or the Romantic notion of the *strange*. As in the case of the German Romanticists, Nerval's mysticism in *Aurélia* is linked with a desire to revive happiness lost on earth—and not with a wish to escape into a completely unfamiliar state of existence: "Quel bonheur de songer que tout ce que nous avons aimé existera toujours autour de nous!"[70] Although his instability of mind opened to him new realms, his verbal technique remained classical.[71] In general it produces dreams and nightmares of an accepted nature, like those in a ghost story or a children's wonderland. For instance the phantom he describes has nothing unusual for a phantom: "Un être d'une grandeur démesurée,—un homme ou femme, je ne sais,—voltigeait péniblement au-dessus de l'espace et semblait se débattre parmi les nuages épais . . ."[72] Later, when he believes that he has entered into the afterworld, he depicts a replica of our own world; not only has human appearance not changed, but even objects have accompanied the dead into paradise through the process of metempsychosis; in speaking of a house which he has recognized in the spiritual sphere, he explains: "Je compris qu'elle avait existé dans je ne sais quel temps, et qu'en ce monde que je visitais alors, le fantôme des

68. *Ibid., Introduction*, p. xi.
69. *Ibid.*, p. 58.
70. *Ibid.*, p. 23.
71. See on the classicism of Nerval: André Rousseaux *Revue Universelle*, XXVIII, 620-6; Kleber Haedens, *Gérard de Nerval*, p. 118.
72. Nerval, *op. cit.*, p. 12.

choses accompagnait celui des corps."[73] He expresses his joy—where the Surrealists would have wept—that the known physical aspects of things are not perishable but symbolic of the spiritual reality which they will attain as they pass through the gates of immortality. "Cela est donc vrai! . . . nous sommes immortels et nous conservons ici les images du monde que nous avons habité. Quel bonheur de songer toujours que tout ce que nous avons aimé existera toujours autour de nous!"[74]

In another dream he locates the "patrie mystique" in his own ancestral mansion, of which he gives a precise and realistic description. He depicts what he is wearing, how he is greeted; he shows himself led by a beautiful woman to the garden; there, again, he enters into a realistic description, naming plants, trees, flowers, in the technical language of the botanist. His dreamworld follows the pattern of our known world except that it is more beautiful. At still another moment Nerval thinks himself transported into another planet. But although he thinks of this new planet as a place of mystical refuge, he brands his vision as that of a madman, stamps it as incredible. And yet what is this new planet? It is a very familiar land; it is the prehistoric world that we have long become accustomed to imagine: full of hideous reptiles, savage vegetation and primitive beings described as monsters. The word "strange" is associated in Nerval's mind with "des palmes gigantesques," "des euphorbes vénéneux," "des acanthes tortillées."[75] It is the weird and mysterious world of the German Romanticists, it is the "strange" of a Théophile Gautier or even of a Huysmans, but not the strange of a Rimbaud, nor of a Surrealist. For his technical classicism did not conform with his abnormal visions, but tended, rather, to reduce them to a plane of realistic imagery.[76] It was thus that Nerval sought to eliminate the contradiction which he sensed between himself and his surroundings.

Finally, when his inner disorder completely distorts for him the harmony of the outer world, Nerval pictures his extraordinary sensations

---

73. *Ibid.*, pp. 22-3.
74. *Ibid.*, p. 23.
75. *Ibid.*, p. 40.
76. What M. Clouard says in reference to Nerval's style in *Voyage en Orient*, could apply to a considerable extent to *Aurélia*: "Du moins est-il certain que le goût de l'humain triomphe, et avec même une intention d'exactitude réaliste," *Voyage en Orient*, I, pp. iii-iv.

as an expiatory prelude to heaven. When his excruciating struggle to overcome his hallucinations or to understand their occult meaning fails and leaves him groping in the semiobscurity of an existence which is neither life nor death, it is to God that he turns for comfort: "Lorsque l'âme flotte incertaine entre la vie et le rêve, entre le désordre de l'esprit et le retour de la froide réflexion, c'est dans la pensée religieuse que l'on doit chercher des secours."[77] But what does "la pensée religieuse" mean to Nerval? Partly pantheistic, partly Christian, his mysticism makes him visualize heaven as the apotheosis of all harmony, of all happiness. The state of existence between two worlds, to which the disorder of his mind has subjected him, is not an aspect of the infinite. On the contrary, it is a state of bondage. If he is overpowered by visions such as those described in *Aurélia*, it is because God has forsaken him. For Nerval, like Lautréamont later on, found God in his own being; but unlike the latter, Nerval associated the *good* in him with God and felt that God had departed from him because he had proved unworthy. As a result, he had experienced a "descente aux enfers,"[78] as he termed his insanity. His literary works were the expression of the anguish which this punishment caused; and the cry with which *Les Filles du feu* terminated: "O Jupiter! quand finira mon supplice?"[79] was answered in *Aurélia* when, after having suffered a "séries d'épreuves,"[80] his heart, which had for so long remained devoid of feeling, refilled with pity. Thus, he entered finally into a state of divine grace.

What Nerval considered "hell" will later be sought out as a plane of existence that disregards the barriers of nature. The type of vision which Nerval believed to be entirely dependent on his mental disorder will be synthetically produced by those who will make it their artistic mission to simulate this irrational state of mind. The dream world which Nerval

---

77. Nerval, *Aurélia*, p. 61.
This same deep religious feeling is evident in the poetry which Hoelderlin wrote at the time of his insanity:

> Die Linen des Lebens sind verschieden,
> Wie Wege sind und wie der Berge Grenzen;
> Was hier wir sind, kann dort ein Gott ergränzen
> Mit Harmonie und ewigen Lohn und Frieden.
> —*Gedichte und Briefe*, p. 201.

78. Nerval, *Aurélia*, p. 118.
79. Nerval, *Les Filles du feu*, p. 393.
80. Nerval, *Aurélia*, p. 118.

hesitated to unravel,[81] the seekers of surreality will invade brazenly. They will have us believe that their work is indeed the expression of one who like Nerval found his soul "distinctement partagée entre la vision et la réalité."[82] But they will set out to represent this state by attempting to evade at the same time both the baroque and the religious concept of the supernatural. And above all they will attempt to devise a language that may be able to express their new vision.

In fine, Romanticism, even in its strangest representations, cannot be said to form the basis of the poetic mysticism that leads to Surrealism. Lautréamont, Rimbaud, Mallarmé, are not "second Romanticists." Rather, they are among the first of a long line of poets and artists who will not only initiate a new literary and artistic technique but contribute as well to the development of a new philosophy. This philosophy will be closely linked with the growth of positivism and at the same time constitute a profound rejection of it.

Romanticism is but a background: a tremendous but passive proscenium arch which will make those who enter upon the scene stand out more distinctly.

81. "le rêve est une second vie. Je n'ai pu percer sans fémir ces portes d'ivoire ou de corne qui nous séparent du monde visible." *Aurélia*, p. 1.
82. *Ibid.*, p. 17.

CHAPTER III

Baudelaire and the Break with Tradition

I

SINCE *Les Fleurs du mal* appeared in 1857 and *Les Paradis artificiels* three years later, it may be said from a purely chronological point of view that Charles Baudelaire's poetic work supplied the transition between the Romanticists and the Symbolist school that dominates the end of the century.

So Jean Pommier regards Baudelaire's poetry and analyses its "mystique."[1] Finding in the "forest of symbols" the basic element of Baudelaire's poetic vision, M. Pommier links this esthetic theory, as best exemplified in the poem "Les Correspondances," with the philosophic ideas of Swedenborg, Diderot, and Lavater, and with the general attitude of the Romanticists toward the physical world. According to this concept the physical aspects of the world correspond to spiritual qualities; the actual appearance of things is the reflection of what is to be revealed in another world. Art would consist of demonstrating the correspondences of the spiritual with the natural, or the influence of the one on the other.

By throwing the spotlight upon this phase of the poetry of Baudelaire, M. Pommier shows, first, the affinities of the author of *Les Fleurs du mal* with the Romanticists and their precursors. He points out, for instance, that Hugo had seen in animals the reflections of the vices and virtues of man, the visible phantoms of the human soul.[2] Likewise, he states, physical nature had symbolized for the Romanticists the various mental states experienced by human nature. Then, by pointing out this same type of analogy and allegory in the poetry of Baudelaire, M.

1. Jean Pommier, *La Mystique de Baudelaire*, Paris, *Les Belles Lettres*, 1932.
2. *Ibid.*, p. 77, he quotes Hugo as saying: "Les animaux ne sont autre chose que les figures de nos vertus et de nos vices, errantes devant nos yeux, les fantômes visibles de nos âmes."

Pommier arrives at the conclusion that: "Baudelaire est de la lignée de Chateaubriand."[3] M. Pommier can now easily proceed from Baudelaire to the Symbolists, for whom all of the physical world exists only as the mirror of the states of the soul and of human ideas. Hence, for the Romanticists as for the Symbolists, nature is a book that can be interpreted even as the Bible: "Le même procédé s'appliquera aux deux 'révélations,' la chrétienne et la spirituelle."[4] Thus, the seekers of the infinite would find the hidden meaning of nature through a system of allegory similar to that of religion: "L'esthétique produit la religion."[5]

In this manner, the poem, "Les Correspondances," through its manifold relations with the Romantic philosophy that preceded it, and through its anticipation of an even greater emphasis on this same poetic attitude, shows Baudelaire as the link in the chain that unites Romanticism with Symbolism in a fundamentally uniform mysticism. Accordingly, "Les Correspondances" is the key poem of Baudelaire and represents the dominant idea of the poetic development of the nineteenth century: "On ne saurait maintenant dénier au sonnet des 'Correspondances' sa valeur unique dans la littérature du XIXᵉ siècle. Il est l'œuvre d'un esprit qui, plus sincèrement peut-être et plus constamment que la plupart de ses contemporains, a pensé selon le mode symboliste."[6]

It is evident that this is an important aspect of Baudelaire's poetry. We know that Baudelaire was acquainted with Swedenborgism. Moreover, M. Pommier's documentation is too exact and his analysis too complete to permit any doubt that this form of allegory has a major place in Les Fleurs du mal. Were this theory of correspondences, however, to encompass the entire literary work of Baudelaire, one could neither be justified in saying that Baudelaire made a break with the old tradition, nor contend that he is in any way the originator of "the great modern tradition" which André Breton[7] dates from Baudelaire's "Voyage:"

3. Pommier, op. cit., p. 86.
4. Ibid., p. 152.
5. Ibid., p. 151.
6. Ibid., p. 154.
7. For an earlier assertion that modernism began with Baudelaire, see Guillaume Apollinaire's preface to the 1917 edition of Baudelaire's Œuvre poétique (J. Chevrel): " . . . En lui s'est incarné pour la première fois l'esprit moderne. C'est à partir de Baudelaire que quelque chose est né qui n'a fait que végéter, tandis que naturalistes, parnassiens, symbolistes passaient auprès sans rien voir, tandis que les naturistes, ayant tourné la tête, n'avaient pas l'audace d'examiner la nouveauté sublime et monstrueuse," p. 3.

Plonger au fond du gouffre, Enfer ou Ciel, qu'importe?
Au fond de l'Inconnu pour trouver du nouveau!

In these lines there are two ideas which do not tie up directly either with the Romanticists or the Symbolists. First, there is the desire to penetrate into the "gouffre" itself rather than be satisfied with nature's intermediary symbols; second, in his pursuit of something entirely new, the poet is willing to risk human and divine values of good and evil: "Enfer ou Ciel, qu'importe." It must be remembered, as M. Pommier himself points out, that "Les Correspondances" were written early in Baudelaire's career. Moreover, if we follow the order Baudelaire gave to his poems, we proceed from this esthetic concept of the infinite to one of another nature: as we reach the poems really entitled "Fleurs du Mal" or those whose headings are "Révolte" or "La Mort," the desire to seek the infinite is no longer a purely mental or esthetic exercise. M. Pommier says the dominant word in Baudelaire's vocabulary is "esprit." Yet, another word becomes increasingly frequent: "gouffre."[8] Beyond the forest of symbols is the entrance to another world; the paths of the forest which man does not fear to tread lead to the River Styx whose unfathomable abysses are foreign to the physical nature that humanity comprehends. "Plonger au fond du gouffre"! For him who dares to say this, there no longer exists a duality in the universe: since the concepts of the natural and the spiritual are both dependent on normal human perceptions, they resolve into a single incomplete reality. To the seeker of complete reality, symbols and the abstractions that they induce are not enough. Feeling himself an exile on earth,[9] the poet will make annotations on "les splendeurs situées derrière le tombeau."[10] and thus, his poetry will become more real than his own existence. In a fragment recently found by Jacques Crépet, entitled "Puisque Réalisme il y a,"

---

8. He was obsessed by this cult of the "gouffre," up to the very last epigraph with which he dedicated his book to those who like him knew how to plunge and suffer in their attempt to find their paradise:

> Mais si, sans se laisser charmer
> Ton œil sait plonger dans les gouffres,
> Lis-moi, pour apprendre à m'aimer;
> Ame curieuse qui souffres
> Et vas cherchant ton paradis,
> Plains-moi . . . Sinon, je te maudis!

> *Les Fleurs du mal.*

9. Cf. Baudelaire, *Nouvelles Histoires extraordinaires,* (NRF) p. 21.
10. *Ibid.,* p. 20.

Baudelaire says: "La poésie est ce qu'il y a de plus réel, c'est ce qui n'est complètement vrai que dans un autre monde."[11]

How will this poetry be more real than human experience? By creating a world in which nature, the barrier to perfect reality, will be robbed of its deceptive characteristics. As has often been pointed out by Baudelaire himself and by many of his critics, he had no feeling for the beauties of nature; he was equally unmoved by the ordinary aspect of human nature. Like the mystical stranger of his little prose poem "L'Etranger," he would recognize no home, no family, no country, save the clouds, the marvelous clouds beyond human grasp.[12] The human and natural world are the "mud" to which he will stoop only to become its master and by his extranatural poetic forces to change into gold.[13]

Two of the controlling factors of nature as conceived by man, are of course, time and place. Often the poet will attempt, therefore, to eliminate these characteristics from the world of his poetry. "Place" will be the symbol of imprisonment on earth, and "heaven" a detachment from the concept of place. One day, while listening to "Lohengrin," Baudelaire felt himself liberated from the laws of gravity and conceived of a soul moving about in luminous nothingness, detached from the natural world:

> Au-dessus des étangs, au-dessus des vallées,
> Des montagnes, des bois, des nuages, des mers,
> Par delà le soleil, par delà les éthers,
> Par delà les confins des sphères étoilées.[14]

"Time" was the other element of which his prison was built. Time to him was one of the most powerful controls that nature exerted on man: "A chaque minute, nous sommes écrasés par l'idée et la sensation du temps."[15] Human activity consisted, consciously or unconsciously, of deceiving Time:

> Faut-il partir? rester? Si tu peux rester, reste;
> Pars, s'il le faut. L'un court, et l'autre se tapit
> Pour tromper l'ennemi vigilant et funeste,
> Le Temps![16]

11. Baudelaire, *Mesure,* 15 juillet, 1938, 4ᵉ année, III, 143.
12. Baudelaire, *Spleen de Paris,* (Librairie Gründ), pp. 164-5.
13. Baudelaire, "Projet de Dédicace," *Œuvres complètes,* (NRF) II, 16.
14. Baudelaire, "Elévation," *Les Fleurs du mal,* p. 13 (Garnier).
15. Baudelaire, "Mon Cœur mis à nu," *Œuvres posthumes,* p. 120.
16. Baudelaire, "Le Voyage," *Les Fleurs du mal,* p. 235.

And the realization of the existence of this yoke makes the plight of human life sadder than that of the vilest animal, according to Baudelaire in "De Profundis Clamavi:"

> *Je jalouse le sort des plus vils animaux*
> *Qui peuvent se plonger dans un sommeil stupide,*
> *Tant l'écheveau du temps lentement se dévide!*[17]

His prose poems such as the one entitled "Enivrez-vous" reflect even more passionately this aspect of the struggle that has to be waged against nature by those who do not wish to be "les martyrisés du Temps."[18] Baudelaire sought out this vigilant and deadly enemy[19] in order to defy and deceive it by conveying an impression of freedom from its laws. In the prose poem "L'Horloge" we have a vision of the absolute hour: ". . . Une heure immobile qui n'est pas marquée sur les horloges, et cependant légère comme un soupir, rapide comme un coup d'œil. Oui, je vois l'heure; il est l'Eternité."[20] It is, in embryonic form, the nonexistent hour within the confines of which Mallarmé's *Igitur* will become a poetic reality. Time is the key that opens and locks the world of the visionary. This is allegorically represented in the curious and very significant prose poem "La Chambre double," whose mystical setting is completely transformed by the mere injection of time into the picture, as if a stage were transfigured by changing nothing but the color of the illumination by a single turn of a switch. The absence of the concept of time had turned this ordinary room into a habitat where every curtain, chair, and table had been stripped of its natural aspect and had become attuned to his desire for the absolute: "Ce que nous nommons généralement la vie même dans son expansion la plus heureuse, n'a rien de commun avec cette vie suprême dont j'ai maintenant connaissance. . . . Non! il n'est plus de minutes, il n'est plus de secondes! Le temps a disparu; c'est l'Eternité qui règne."[21]

Then there enters into his unearthly solitude a bailiff, the most earthly and concrete example of despicable humanity—and the spell

17. *Ibid.*, p. 50.
18. Baudelaire, *Spleen de Paris*, p. 226.
19. See note 16.
20. Baudelaire, *Spleen de Paris*, p. 226.
21. *Ibid.*, pp. 167-9.

is broken. The first evidence of the poet's return to ordinary life is the resumption of the ticking of the clock, which seems to say:

> *Je suis la Vie, l'insupportable, l'implacable Vie!!.......Oui!*
> *le Temps règne; il a repris sa brutale dictature.*[21]

He cries out: "Horreur! je me souviens! je me souviens!"[21] For it is of memory that Time's chain is made; it is the instrument by which Time wields its power. Baudelaire, however, who in many other instances had prided himself on being able to evoke at his will a thousand happy moments out of the past, was never to carry his revolt against the concept of time to the point of rejecting the faculty of remembering. On the contrary, memory supplied the substance of most of his visions.

Baudelaire's attempt to seek out "un mystère divin que l'homme n'entend pas,"[22] of which there is a leitmotiv throughout his poetry, is crystallized into a final expression, which he called "Le Voyage" but which ironically is the very repudiation of voyage and marks the end of a poetic millenium. In 1859, in a letter to Charles Asselineau, Baudelaire spoke of his dedication of this poem to Maxime du Camp in the following terms: "J'ai fait un long poème dédié à Maxime du Camp, qui est à faire frémir la nature, et surtout les amateurs du progrès."[23] How had he proposed to make nature tremble? He had laughed at nature by making it seem unable to satisfy man's consummate desire to know and experience. At the same time he had chided man for consenting to let the limits of the seas stunt the boundless possibilities that his dreams opened to him:

> *Et nous allons, suivant le rythme de la lame.*
> *Berçant notre infini sur le fini des mers:*[24]

In this instance the sea, far from being the symbol of the poet's passion for the infinite, is put in sharp contrast to it. Baudelaire had injected in his poem a cynical pity for those whom he had pictured as ostensibly deriving pleasure from voyage, but who roll like the top and ball, jostled by a curiosity which drives them like madmen, makes them dream of the undescribable only to awake to the realization that Imagination was incapable of making good its promises:

22. Baudelaire, *Œuvres complètes,* II, 36.
23. *Ibid.,* II, 424.
24. Baudelaire, *Les Fleurs du mal,* pp. 230-1.

L'imagination qui dresse son orgie
Ne trouve qu'un récif aux clartés du matin.[24]

Although they be not only discoverers but drunken inventors of Americas, what can these travellers tell us to alleviate the boredom of our imprisonment? One pose of nature is identical with every other:

Amer savoir, celui qu'on tire du voyage.
Le monde, monotone et petit, aujourd'hui,
Hier, demain, toujours, nous fait voir notre image,
Une oasis d'horreur dans un désert d'ennui![25]

The only way to cheat time and place, the only way to defy nature, is through the voyage into the infinite, the voyage to Death: But what is death? Is it "le portique ouvert sur les Cieux inconnus,!"[26] or is death a terrible awakening to the fact that it is nothing different, nothing new, as in the "Rêve d'un Curieux":

J'étais mort, sans surprise, et la terrible aurore
M'enveloppait.—Eh quoi! n'est-ce donc que cela!
La toile était levée et j'attendais encore.[27]

Is this typical of a man who seeks in the mystical the counterpart of the physical or vice versa? The emptiness, the bareness, the blackness that he wished to experience might prove after all but a continuation of the familiar world from which he was trying to wrench himself:

Mais les ténèbres sont elles-mêmes des toiles
Où vivent, jaillissant de mon œil par milliers,
Des êtres disparus aux regards familiers.[28]

Unlike the Romanticists, who expected to find in death final and complete compensation for earthly dissatisfactions, Baudelaire, despite his call to Death, was too much the skeptic to expect to find in it the freedom he sought. He was obsessed by the idea of a "gouffre,"[29] but this abyss did not necessarily signify death or the

25. *Ibid.*, pp. 235-6.
26. *Ibid.*, "La Mort des pauvres," p. 226.
27. *Ibid.*, "Rêve d'un curieux," p. 229.
28. *Ibid.*, "Obsession," p. 122.
29. See *Mon Cœur mis à nu, Œuvres posthumes*, p. 119.

"au-delà." He used "gouffre" synonymously with "infini." In his mind this "infinite" did not, I think, take any religious form, but, on the contrary, was accompanied at times by an irreligious attitude. According to the travellers who are questioned in "Le Voyage" they were met everywhere on their journeys with the spectacle of:

> *Plusieurs religions semblables à la nôtre,*
> *Toutes escaladant le ciel;*[30]

None of these religions seems to explain the unknown that the poet seeks. Hence his contempt for the race of Abel, content to sleep, drink, and eat under divine protection,[31] without wishing anything further. Rather is he attracted to the revolt of Caïn and to the perversities which constitute its nature. Caïn and his master, Satan, represent a conglomeration of the disorders of nature: perversion of spirituality, perversion of morality. But since Satan knows the secrets of the universe, the poet calls him "Bâton des exilés, lampe des inventeurs"[32] and demands of him:

> *Fais que mon âme un jour, sous l'Arbre de Science,*
> *Près de toi se repose, à l'heure où sur ton front*
> *Comme un Temple nouveau ses rameaux s'épandront.*[33]

Thus, the abyss of evil, generally associated with inferno, is linked in the poet's mind with his passion to know the infinite. He who would say "Je ne vois qu'infini par toutes les fenêtres"[34] in a poem entitled "Le Gouffre," elsewhere calls himself:

> *. . . ennemi des familles,*
> *Favori de l'enfer,*[35]

and he pursues the infinite through a defiance of normal sensations and emotions. Just as "Le Reniement de Saint Pierre," "Abel et Caïn," and "Les Litanies de Satan" are a revolt against normal religion, so "Lesbos" and "Les Femmes Damnées" defy natural love. The "femmes damnées" are "chercheuses d'infini" because their revolt against nature's laws has detached them from the world gov-

---

30. Baudelaire, "Le Voyage," *Les Fleurs du mal*, p. 234.
31. *Ibid.*, "Abel et Caïn," pp. 217-8.
32. *Ibid.*, "Les Litanies de Satan," p. 221.
33. *Ibid.*, "Prière," p. 221.
34. *Ibid.*, "Le Gouffre," p. 268.
35. *Ibid.*, "Les Deux Bonnes Sœurs," p. 201.

erned by order: "Que nos rideaux fermés nous séparent du monde,"[36] is their desire. Therefore, the poet addresses them as follows:

> *O vierges, ô démons, ô monstres, ô martyres,*
> *De la réalité grands esprits contempteurs,*
> *Chercheuses d'infini, dévotes et satyres,*
> *Vous que dans votre enfer mon âme a poursuivies.*[37]

Thus the voyage to the Absolute ended in hell; thus extreme, unconditional mysticism was accompanied in certain poems of Baudelaire with the first symptoms of the characteristics so evident in the Surrealists: an anti-social, anti-natural tendency coupled with a will to destroy obvious and accepted human values.[38] It is the road that we shall see Lautréamont take—by which he will arrive at his aberrations and his cult of evil—the same road which Rimbaud will take in his Journey to Hell, the same that a long line of poets will explore in their efforts to revitalize poetry.

II

> —*Et les moins sots, hardis amants de la Démence,*
> *Fuyant le grand troupeau parqué par le Destin,*
> *Et se réfugiant dans l'opium immense!*
> —*Tel est du globe entier l'éternel bulletin.*
>
> —*"Le Voyage"*

The visions which Gérard de Nerval had experienced through his abnormality, Baudelaire attempted to achieve through the "dose [quota-allotment] of opium" which he believed each human being to possess by nature, and which could be incessantly renewed.[39] Poetry was to be the stimulus which might keep him in a constant state of rapture, and through which alone he would know the other face of reality. However, the natural grain of opium by which Charles Baudelaire sought his infinite was not enough to bring him

36. *Ibid.*, "Femmes Damnées," p. 197.
37. *Ibid.*, p. 200.
38. See also "La Destruction," *Ibid.*, p. 187.
39. Baudelaire, "Invitation au voyage," *Spleen de Paris*, p. 191: "Chaque homme porte en lui sa dose d'opium naturel, incessamment secrétée et renouvelée."

a complete vision. His poetry, despite all evidences it gives of taking new directions, seldom reveals in its general classical outline the technique by which a representation of the irrational might be achieved by the poet. *Les Fleurs du mal* and *Spleen de Paris* are a break with tradition in thought but not in form. When Baudelaire spoke of the wish to: "allonger les heures par l'infini des sensations,"[40] or of finding his black tulip or blue dahlia,[40] he gave no more the impression of realizing his wish than did Novalis of really having found his blue flower or George Sand her blue rose. In "Les Dons des fées" he defied the common reasoners and flaunted the logic of the absurd (by which later poets were to live) but gave no sustained illustration of it; he contented himself rather with a complaint against "ces raisonneurs si communs, incapables de s'élever jusqu'à la logique de l'Absurde."[41] Baudelaire's interest in the irrational in thought and the abnormal in sensation led him to an investigation of the artificial paradises of opium and hashish. His *Paradis artificiels* are not a confession like De Quincey's, nor a search for happiness like Gautier's,[42] but an active exploration of orgy through an intent absorption akin to that of the ascetic.[43]

Baudelaire was fully cognizant of the universal nature of the attraction of drugs: "Cette acuité de la pensée, cet enthousiasme des sens et de l'esprit ont dû, en tout temps, apparaître à l'homme comme le premier des biens."[44] He saw as the main reason for this attraction the desire for flight, the search for "les moyens de fuir,"[45] the ambition to find Paradise in one short step.[46] He regarded the experience of the hashish taker as a strange journey, more enticing than ordinary voyages because of its unknown destination. "La vapeur a sifflé, la voiture est orientée, et vous avez sur les voyageurs ordinaires ce curieux privilège d'ignorer où vous allez. Vous l'avez voulu; vive la fatalité."[47] But together with an initial curiosity in this voyage, which has a great deal in common with the inner voyage of later poets, there is in Baudelaire's attitude an element of fear; there

---

40. *Ibid.*, pp. 190-1.
41. *Ibid.*, p. 195.
42. Gautier, Théophile, *Le Club des Haschischins.*
43. Cf. J. Baruzi, *Volonté de Métamorphose*, p. 55 for comparison of the addict and the ascetic.
44. Baudelaire, *Les Paradis artificiels*, p. 36.
45. *Ibid.*, p. 37.
46. *Ibid.*, p. 37.
47. *Ibid.*, p. 45.

appear certain misgivings; he characterizes the experience as "Epouvantable mariage de l'homme avec lui-même,"[48] and he is afraid that the will that drives him toward these inner resources may be overcome by the powers it discovers. In his scale of values the possession of his free will ranks above the ability to flee into an artificial paradise: "La volonté surtout est attaquée, de toutes les facultés la plus précieuse."[49] If he is to experience new visions, they must be voluntarily created; we have here the same Baudelaire who in his poetry had said:

> Architecte de mes féeries
> Je faisais à ma volonté
> Sous un tunnel de pierreries
> Passer un océan dompté.[50]

To him, what robbed man of his intelligence and freedom of action (no matter how limited that action might be) was not a true means of escape but on the contrary a state of slavery. Time and again he used the expression "esclave" to characterize the drug addict and called him a deplorably sick man.

In this respect his tone is reminiscent of De Quincey's, who wrote in his Confessions of an Opium Eater of the "accursed chains which fettered" him,[51] of the "vassalage"[52] that opium brought about, and who described Coleridge as a "slave of opium."[52] But if in attitude De Quincey may be considered a precursor of Baudelaire, I do not agree with those who find that Les Paradis artificiels are for the most part a translation or adaptation of the Confessions.[53]

In De Quincey's experience with opium, self-possession and serenity remained and were even reinforced under the influence of the drug. What gave him happiness in his opium dreams was the fact that his pleasures were mostly intellectual. The Asiatic dreams he had were based, even when horrible for the senses to experience, upon his knowledge of the Orient. When he went to hear the famous Grassini sing after he had taken the drug, his appreciation of the music was enhanced by his increased activity of mind:

48. Ibid., p. 62.
49. Ibid., p. 74.
50. Baudelaire, Les Fleurs du mal, "Rêve parisien," p. 167-8.
51. Thomas De Quincey, The Collected Writings, III, 211.
52. Ibid., pp. 229-31.
53. Cf. Randolph Hughes, "Vers la contrée du rêve," Mercure de France, 1ᵉʳ août, p. 578.

It is by the reaction of the mind upon the notices of the ear (the matter coming by the senses, the *form* from the mind) that the pleasure is constructed; and therefore it is that people of equally good ear differ so much in this point from one another. Now opium, by greatly increasing the activity of the mind, generally increases of necessity, that particular mode of its activity by which we are able to construct out of the raw material of organic sound an elaborate intellectual pleasure.[54]

To Baudelaire, however, the transformations operated by drugs were for the most part of a sensory nature. It was not his concepts but his perceptions that were metamorphosed. In De Quincey's *Confessions* the only distortion of perspective was indicated by his sensing of an "expansion" of time and space:

The sense of space, and in the end the sense of time, were both powerfully affected. Buildings, landscapes, etc. were exhibited in proportions so vast as the bodily eye is not fitted to receive. Space swelled, and was amplified to an extent of unutterable and self-repeating infinity. This disturbed me very much less than the vast expansion of time. Sometimes I seemed to have lived for seventy or a hundred years in one night; nay, sometimes had feelings representative of a duration far beyond the limits of any human experience.[55]

This sensation of "expansion," which De Quincey classed among the *Pains of Opium,* is supposed to be the most potent power of opium, as analysed in the *Confessions,* and supplies the link between De Quincey and Baudelaire. But whereas every literary analysis of the drug addict from De Quincey and Gautier to Baruzi[56] has indicated this change in the concept of time and space, and has described other basic distortions and transpositions of perception, everyone has given logical accounts of the illogical phenomena. Gautier went so far as to lose consciousness at a most convenient moment: just as he reached the most interesting aspect of the hallucination.

Baudelaire explained early in *Les Paradis artificiels* that human beings could experience two kinds of dreams: the natural and the "sur-

54. De Quincey, *op. cit.,* pp. 390-1.
55. *Ibid.,* p. 435.
56. See note 43 on Baruzi.

naturel;" he expected from the effects of hashish no more than
the intensification and expansion of normal sensations that other
drug addicts had experienced: "le grossissement, la déformation et
l'exagération de ses sentiments habituels et de ses perceptions mo-
rales, qui présentent alors, dans une atmosphère exceptionnelle, un
véritable phénomène de réfraction."[57] On the other hand, the "surnaturel" according to him, could only be sensed in a dream which
had no relation to man's ordinary life, but which was steeped in absurdities:

> Les rêves de l'homme sont de deux classes. Les uns, pleins de
> sa vie ordinaire, de ses préoccupations, de ses désirs, ses vices,
> se combinent d'une façon plus ou moins bizarre avec les objets
> entrevus dans la journée, qui se sont indiscrètement fixés sur la
> vaste toile de sa mémoire. Voilà le rêve naturel; il est l'homme
> lui-même. Mais l'autre espèce de rêve! le rêve absurde, im-
> prévu, sans rapport ni connexion avec le caractère, la vie et les
> passions du dormeur! ce rêve, que j'appellerai hiéroglyphique,
> représente évidemment le côté surnaturel de la vie, et c'est
> justement parce qu'il est absurde que les anciens l'ont cru
> divin. . . .[58]

He did not expect to sense nor convey through his hashish visions
this absurdity, which he was inclined to call "divine:" "Dans l'ivresse
du haschisch, rien de semblable. Nous ne sortirons pas du rêve
naturel."[58] And yet, Baudelaire's representation of his hallucinations
resulted in an imagery which came closer to this idea of the "surnaturel" than the dream transcriptions of his predecessors.

In both De Quincey's *Confessions* and Baudelaire's *Paradis artificiels*
there is the account of a spectacle witnessed under the effect of drugs.
While De Quincey experiences just an expansion of his normal intellectual appreciation of the performance, in *Les Paradis artificiels* the
scene is entirely transfigured. Instead of an intellectual expansion,
we observe a deviation by which the mind of the hashish eater es-
capes from the ordinary spectacle and creates another based on a
new logic which puts disconnected ideas together to produce a
credible whole:

57. Baudelaire, *Les Paradis artificiels,* p. 62.
58. *Ibid.,* p. 43.

Je ne vous dirai pas que j'écoutais les comédiens, vous savez que cela est impossible; de temps en temps ma pensée accrochait au passage un lambeau de phrase, et, semblable à une danseuse habile, elle s'en servait comme d'un tremplin pour bondir dans des rêveries très lointaines. On pourrait supposer qu'un drame, entendu de cette façon, manque de logique et d'enchaînement: détrompez-vous, je découvrais un sens très subtil dans le drame créé par ma distraction.[59]

What appears to us irrational is perfectly rational in the new perspective. The transformation is not purely intellectual; he seems to see this strange drama through a stereoscope: "Quant à la scène (c'était une scène consacrée au genre comique), elle seule était lumineuse, infiniment petite et située loin, très loin, comme au bout d'un immense stéréoscope."[59] Yet, infinitesimal and far away though everything appears, a new acuteness and a change of sensory values make him notice the small unimportant details with the greatest clarity to the exclusion of the more obvious elements, such as the action and gestures and the quality of the voice, upon which the ordinary audience would be centering its attention.

Les comédiens me semblaient excessivement petits et cernés d'un contour précis et soigné, comme les figures de Meissonier. Je voyais distinctement, non seulement les détails les plus minutieux de leurs ajustements . . . mais encore la ligne de séparation du faux front d'avec le véritable, le blanc, le bleu et le rouge, et tous les moyens de grimage. Et ces liliputiens étaient revêtus d'une clarté froide et magique, comme celle qu'une vitre très nette ajoute à une peinture à l'huile.[60]

It is the triumph of the detail, not by its quantity (as in Gautier's descriptions) but by its change of rank. It is the initial step of what José Ortega y Gasset later was to call an element of the "dehumanization" in the new art: an "infrarealism" which he describes as an evasion of reality through the overemphasis of details which tend to distort familiar perceptions.[61] Baudelaire's artificial paradise is the first step toward the world of the Surrealists, in which the small

59. Baudelaire, *Les Paradis artificiels,* p. 53.
60. *Ibid.,* pp. 53-4.
61. José Ortega y Gasset, *The Dehumanization of Art.*

part was to become more significant than the whole by defying nature's forms and perspectives.

Gradually freeing themselves from recording natural forms, the senses become more and more keen, seek the infinite and seem to create their own objects:

> C'est en effet à cette période de l'ivresse que se manifeste une finesse nouvelle, une acuité supérieure dans tous les sens. L'odorat, la vue, l'ouïe, le toucher participent également à ce progrès. Les yeux visent l'infini. L'oreille perçoit des sons insaisissables au milieu du plus vaste tumulte. C'est alors que commencent les hallucinations. Les objets extérieurs prennent lentement, successivement, des apparences singulières; ils se déforment et se transforment. Puis arrivent les équivoques, les méprises et les transpositions d'idées. Les sons se revêtent de couleurs, et les couleurs contiennent de la musique.[62]

This is not a "correspondence" but a distortion of nature. Continuing his explanation of the effects of hashish, Baudelaire shows how his sensations finally surpass human characteristics and enter into the realm of mathematical abstraction.

> Les notes musicales deviennent des nombres, et si votre esprit est doué de quelque aptitude mathématique, la mélodie, l'harmonie écoutée . . . se transforme en une vaste opération arithmétique, où les nombres engendrent les nombres, et dont vous suivez les phases et la génération avec une facilité inexplicable.[63]

The abnormality of this new world lies not in the visions of the horrible and grotesque as with De Quincey but in a complete change of point of view; as in the case of Nerval and of later poets who are included in this study, there often occurs a detachment from human personality and an objective association of oneself with one's visions.[64]

62. Baudelaire, *op. cit.*, p. 54.
63. *Ibid.*, p. 54.
64. Even before Baudelaire, Théophile Gautier conveys a little of this same impression:
> Par un prodige bizarre, au bout de quelques minutes de contemplation, je me fondais dans l'objet fixe et je devenais moi-même cet objet.

Club des Haschischins, (1846) p. 489

> Il arrive quelquefois que la personnalité disparaît et que l'objectivité, qui est le propre des poètes panthéistes, se développe en vous si anormalement que la contemplation des objets extérieurs vous fait oublier votre propre existence, et que vous vous confondez bientôt avec eux.[65]

It is through this process that a new type of reality will be created in which comparisons, metaphors come to be considered by the artist as actual realities rather than literary representations of perceptions. It brings about an almost complete transmutation of the "I," an escape from the human form itself; it produces the complete dehumanization that José Ortega y Gasset notes in modern art. Baudelaire describes it as follows:

> Votre œil se fixe sur un arbre harmonieux courbé par le vent; dans quelques secondes, ce qui ne serait dans le cerveau d'un poète qu'une comparaison fort naturelle deviendra dans la vôtre une réalité. Vous prêtez d'abord à l'arbre vos passions, votre désir ou votre mélancolie; ses gémissements, et ses oscillations deviennent vôtres, et bientôt vous êtes l'arbre. De même l'oiseau qui plane au fond de l'azur représente d'abord l'immortelle envie de planer au-dessus des choses humaines; mais déjà vous êtes l'oiseau lui-même.[66]

This evolution which Baudelaire seems to have analyzed as an essential transformation of the subject into the object under the influence of hashish is comparable also in some respect to the evolution of poetry from Symbolism, with its reliance on representation, to Surrealism which will sacrifice the representation if needs be, in its effort to come to grips with the essence of reality.

Baudelaire's artificial paradise is not the world of the fantastic or baroque or supernatural which the works of Maturin, Lewis, and Borel had been putting in vogue. Baudelaire's is not the experience of the ordinary addict. His already over-subtle senses had found here the very darkest reaches of the "gouffre" he was seeking to explore, a "roman fantastique,"[67] a constant change and renewal of personality at its source. Yet with the passing of the effects of the

---

65. Baudelaire, *op. cit.*, pp. 54-5.
66. *Ibid.*, p. 55.
67. *Ibid.*, p. 55.

drug, Baudelaire saw himself thrown back upon hideous nature: "La hideuse nature, dépouillée de son illumination de la veille, ressemble aux mélancoliques débris d'une fête."[68]

Many who read his work were to simulate his short-lived paradise. Some like Antoine Monnier[69] were to explore the same world of hashish. Others, like Arthur Rimbaud, were to create to an even greater degree the same illumination without making it dependent on artificial stimuli. Baudelaire's "roman fantastique" was to become Rimbaud's "opéra fabuleux," but the latter was to be a "voyant" in the technical sense of the word, as used by the hashish eaters: an adept who retains his own sobriety while aiding to create and control the hallucinations of others.[70] For if *Les Paradis artificiels* is significant as a literary source, it is because this work was more than the transcription of hashish dreams. In it, Baudelaire had exercised—perhaps unconsciously—the two literary "qualities" which he considered "fundamental," and out of which was to arise the technique of those to follow him: "Deux qualités littéraires fondamentales: surnaturalisme et ironie. Coup d'œil individuel, aspect dans lequel se tiennent les choses devant l'écrivain, puis tournure d'esprit satanique."[71] These are the bases of his "modernism." By perceiving objects in an independent way and interpreting them through a satanic turn of mind, his successors will attempt to transform completely the old Romantic themes and will create a new poetic mysticism.

68. *Ibid.*, p. 74.
69. How much better than most of his contemporaries Monnier understood the essence of Baudelaire's poetry! Dedicating his *Haschisch* to the poet of *Les Fleurs du mal*, he wrote in 1877:

> A l'ombre de celui qui fit les *Fleurs du mal*
> Au poète du spleen qui, de l'impossible ivre,
> Poussa jusqu'au hideux la haine du banal,
> Je dédie humblement les rimes de ce livre.

70. It seems to me that Rimbaud derived his title of *Les Illuminations* from *Les Paradis artificiels* and the concept of the "voyant" from Gautier's explanation. of its meaning in hashish terminology: "on appelle ainsi l'adepte sobre," p. 487, rather than from more remote sources.
71. Baudelaire, *Fusées*, p. 81.

CHAPTER IV

A Spiritual Crisis

THE CHANGE in the mysticism of the French poet in the course of the nineteenth century was not an isolated accident but had its basis in the general spiritual crisis caused by the repercussions of Auguste Comte's positivism and by the physiological experimentation that dominated the second half of the century. Mysticism, be it in poetry or philosophy, had up to then either sought to explain the lower by the higher forms of existence, or failing this, had believed in a definite schism between man and the other forms of life. In the eighteenth century, despite the theories that La Mettrie had advanced on the purely mechanical aspects of the human structure, or Maupertuis' allocation of the power to reason within the atom, it was the concept of the "Great Chain of Being" that had had the greatest attraction for the philosophers of that Age of Enlightenment. The advocates of this theory did not see in the animal the composite of all the characteristics of man but rather perceived in the entire series of living things successive attempts of Nature to create a more perfect form. Those who believed in such a chain of being, stretching from the "néant" to the infinite, attributed, in reduced quantities, human physical and moral characteristics to the lower forms; since the proportion between nothingness and infinity was entirely different for the inferior forms of life, man's belief in his superiority was not shaken as it was to be later with the advent of Darwinism.

The poetry of the Romanticists was to be based primarily on this eighteenth-century concept of the "great chain of being"; as E. Spenlé points out in his very comprehensive study of Novalis, the Romanticists had seen in the lower forms the first drafts of the higher forms of life.[1] The plant strove toward the animal, the ani-

1. See *Supra,* note 22, Chap. II.

mal toward man, and man toward God. As has been indicated
earlier in this study, this is certainly the ladder which French Romantic poetry utilized; it is just such a gradation that Hugo gives
to the characters of his poem "Dieu"; according to their relative
level, animal, man, and angel plod their way toward the discovery
of the infinite.

By 1845, however, Auguste Comte had established in the minds
of men the possibility of a new order of things: he had placed man
within the order of physiochemical phenomena. Life was no longer
to be considered a *series* of patterns but one pattern rendered more
and more intricate. With the publication in 1859 of Darwin's *The
Origin of Species,* and in 1865 of Claude Bernard's *Introduction à
l'étude de la médecine expérimentale* the study of human nature
seemed to have been brought closer and closer to that of physics
and chemistry, while the study of metaphysics appeared to become
entirely irrelevant to an understanding of man; for now the highest beings in the universe were to be explained by the "mouvement
mécanique" of the lowest.[2] Such a concept tended to dislodge the
entire concept of metaphysics. *L'Avenir de la Science* was already
written by 1848, and in it Renan had considered science the only
legitimate means of acquiring knowledge; he attributed the hold
that religions had had on humanity in the past to their quasi-scientific character: their ability to "exercise" the human mind.

By the 1860's both the scientists and philosophers had exaggerated and distorted the contentions of positivism. In 1865, Paul
Janet, writing of the prevalent philosophical and scientific opinions
in a work entitled *Crise philosophique,* says: ". . . l'école spiri-
tualiste a subi depuis dix ou quinze ans un échec des plus graves."[3]
A few years later in an article on "La Nouvelle Philosophie de la
nature" Charles Lévêque describes an even more critical situation:
"Dans ces dernières années, le crédit de cette science (métaphysique)
des causes a paru gravement compromis. De tous les points de
l'horizon des ennemis se sont levés contre elle. Cet assaut général
était de nature à ébranler les convictions les plus éprouvées."[4] The

2. E. Vacherot, "La Science et la Conscience," *Revue des Deux-Mondes*
LXXXI, 84-5.

3. P. Janet, *Crise philosophique,* p. 6.

4. C. Lévêque, "La Nouvelle Philosophie de la nature," *Revue des Deux-
Mondes,* LXXXI, 598.

conflict took the form of violent polemics between clergy and lay-man, philosopher and scientist. In the years 1868-9 there appeared in the *Revue des Deux-Mondes* alone more articles pertaining to this struggle than to any other matter; the most eminent intellects of the time and the most representative of the journalists of the epoch took part in the dispute over science and conscience, materialism and mysticism, positivism and idealism.[5] There seemed to be no more room for metaphysical speculation now that the gaps in sci-entific knowledge were being more and more rapidly filled; as na-ture took an increasingly organized appearance, it was eliminating the supernatural, and the miracle was yielding all its ground to science.[6]

It is common knowledge, of course, that by the end of the cen-tury there arose a strong reaction against the entire concept of pos-itivism. But the first attempts at conciliation had appeared as early as the 1840's. The mathematician Cournot had criticized his con-temporary Auguste Comte for seeming to attribute to reason an un-warranted importance. His findings in the field of mathematical chance had revealed to him that certain phenomena had an under-lying cause but did not thereby enter within the orbit of reason. The human mind, accustomed to seek from earliest childhood the reason for things, was confronted with the unpredictable character-istics of chance, for which no reasonable explanation could be found. In the face of what Mallarmé some years later described as: "l'unique nombre qui ne peut pas être un autre," Cournot began to question the supremacy given to reason by his contemporary Au-guste Comte. Other mathematical findings made by him replace the old notion of "zéro" or "néant" by the notion of the "infiniment petit." Mathematically a unit could be made progressively smaller without ever having to reach the arbitrary zero point. Not the suc-cessive numbers, but this general movement of the gradually di-minishing unit, which would never reach zero, seemed to make the concept of eternity enter within the orbit of logic. Cournot called

5. In the *Revue des Deux-Mondes,* of 1868 and 1869 are at least 15 articles with titles such as "La Science et la Religion," "La Science et la Conscience," "Philosophie et Religion," "Le Spiritualisme dans la science," "La Crise re-ligieuse au 19ᵉ siècle," "Le Spiritualisme français au 19ᵉ siècle," etc.

6. See A. Reveille, "Le Sentiment religieux," *Revue des Deux-Mondes,* LXXXI, 903.

this liaison between science and metaphysics "le transrationnel," which implied: "passer au travers de la raison, non la briser."[7]

In his *L'Avenir de la Science* Renan envisaged something of the same order, when in view of scientific discoveries, he looked forward to the future acceptance of an "infini réel" superior to the older concept of the "infini métaphysique."

In the 1860's when the religious and irreligious factions were at the height of their "luttes aussi bruyantes que stériles,"[8] it was this very idea that suggested a compromise between positivism and mysticism to scientifically inclined philosophers and to philosophically inclined scientists. A. Reveille recognized in the conflict of the time the symptoms of "une évolution nouvelle de la science religieuse"[9] in 1869. In the same year another contributor to the *Revue des Deux-Mondes* asked the question: "Peut-on, s'élevant des choses tangibles et des mouvements aux forces et des forces à un principe psychique, fonder le spiritualisme sur la science elle-même?"[10] By 1870, two channels were suggested as outlets for a mysticism that would be in keeping with the scientific attitude: 1) a renewal of Platonic idealism: God existing only in thought, perfection being realized solely in the realm of abstract concepts; 2) a mysticism based on a new conception of materialism, a spiritual perception rising out of the physical stimuli of the senses. Positivism did not deny the infinite, pointed out Paul Janet, quoting from Littré's *Paroles de philosophie positiviste:*

> Ce qui est au-delà . . . est absolument inaccessible à l'esprit humain; mais inaccessible ne veut pas dire nul ou non existant. L'immensité, tant matérielle qu'intellectuelle, tient par un lien étroit à nos connaissances, et devient par cette alliance une idée positive du même ordre; je veux dire que, en les touchant et en les bordant, cette immensité apparaît sous son double carac-

7. Jean de La Harpe, *De l'Ordre et du hasard,* Université de Neuchâtel, *Mémoires,* 1936, IX, 188. In this dissertation M. de La Harpe gives a synthesis of the entire work of Antoine Augustin Cournot. The above brief exposé of Cournot's theories is based on La Harpe.

8. A. Reveille, *op. cit.,* p. 903.

9. *Ibid.,* p. 906.

10. Auguste Langel, "Le Spiritualisme dans la science," *Revue des Deux-Mondes,* LXXXI, 442.

tère, la réalité et l'inaccessibilité. C'est un océan qui vient battre notre rive, et pour lequel nous n'avons ni barques ni voiles, mais dont la claire vision est aussi salutaire que formidable.[11]

Although the cosmos was inaccessible to the human mind, it existed in the form of innumerable atoms such as those within human range. Speaking of the past "spiritualisme français," Paul Janet found that: "Il a montré Dieu hors du monde et le monde hors de Dieu, il n'a pas assez montré Dieu dans le monde et le monde en Dieu."[12] By trying to show, on the contrary, God *in* the material world, man could raise matter to the level of the spirit rather than lower the mind to that of matter—as a superficial understanding of materialism would imply.

A little later in 1887 there appeared a monumental work by M. Guyau, entitled *L'Irréligion de l'avenir*,[13] which seemed to crystallize the materialistic mysticism of the times:

> Etre irréligieux ou a-religieux n'est pas être anti-religieux. Bien plus . . . l'irréligion de l'avenir pourra garder du sentiment religieux ce qu'il y avait en lui de plus pur: d'une part l'admiration du Cosmos et des puissances infinies qui y sont déployées; d'autre part, la recherche d'un idéal non seulement individuel, mais social et même cosmique, qui dépasse la réalité actuelle.[14]

He seemed to anticipate the surrealist notion that through an abnegation of positive religion the spiritual curiosity of man might become more acute.[15]

By the end of the century it was generally accepted by science and philosophy that the apparent defeat of metaphysics by positivism had neither killed the notion of the "Inconnaissable" nor the idea of the infinite. On the centenary of the birth of Auguste Comte,

11. P. Janet, "Philosophie et Religion," *Revue des Deux-Mondes*, LXXXI, 350.

12. Janet, "Le Spiritualisme français," *Revue des Deux-Mondes*, LXXV, 383.

13. In 1890 Ad. Franck in *Nouveaux Essais de critique philosophique* considered this work of Guyau perhaps the only one that would give to future generations a true picture of the times as far as speculative tendencies were concerned. See p. 164.

14. M. Guyau, *L'Irréligion de l'avenir*, p. xiv.

15. *Ibid.*, pp. xviii-ix.

Brunetière emphasized the fact that Comte, while delving into the laws governing various types of phenomena, had not ventured to expose the generating causes of these phenomena. On the contrary positivism had limited its activities to the realm of relative things, and by so doing, it had implied the existence of the "nonrelatif," or absolute. And by accepting the concept of the absolute, science had sanctioned religion.[16]

At the same time, in almost the same words, Janet, developing his earlier reasoning, was explaining to his students that, although for a number of years the idea of God had disappeared from philosophy, it really formed an integral part of human thought. The finite implied the infinite: the infinite is bounded either by something or nothing; if by nothing, it is then the infinite itself; if it is bounded by something, then it is a relative finite: "Qui dit relatif dit absolu. Une chose ne peut être relative que par rapport à une autre chose qui ne l'est pas, et qui par conséquent est absolue."[17]

Moreover, science itself was much more on its guard by the end of the century than it had been previously. Henri Poincaré asserted that there were two equal necessities in the human intellect: to understand the finite and to envisage the expanses of the infinite. Science only claimed to comprehend exterior aspects of things, and therefore had no connection with the infinite.[18]

Finally in the field of philosophy it was of course Henri Bergson who attempted the most definite conciliation between science and mysticism. Through what he called "évolution créatrice," he sought to understand within matter those spontaneous qualities which resisted logical laws, and by means of the scientific method he wished to determine the existence of mental qualities beyond the known cerebral activities of man.[19]

What kinship was there between this philosophic crisis and the evolution of art? This spiritual crisis had its counterpart in the artistic development of the age, and particularly in poetry. The "Parnasse," in its quasi-scientific precision and reasonableness, its preoc-

16. F. Brunetière, "Pour le Centenaire d'Auguste Comte," pamphlet, Tome IX, 1902, pp. 679-92.
17. See Janet, *Principes de métaphysique et de psychologie:* leçons professées à la Faculté des lettres de Paris (1888-94) pp. 91-8.
18. Henri Poincaré, "Conceptions nouvelles de la matière," *Le Matérialisme actuel,* (1913), pp. 51-67.
19. H. Bergson, "L'Ame et le Corps," *Ibid.*

cupation with exterior reality and its resignation to the "néant" as
the last outposts of intellectual activity, had corresponded to the
acute positivism immediately following the recognition of the theories of Auguste Comte. Moreover, naturalism might be said to represent in the realm of literature the misunderstanding and exagger-
ation of positivism. On the other hand, much of the symbolism of
1885 was a reflection of the irreligion which satiates its craving for
the mystical in a rarefaction of nature and sensation through the
process of abstraction.

But from 1867 on, another point of view was to be taken by a
certain number of poets. Accepting a compromise between materialism and metaphysics, they were to develop a mysticism based on the
total acceptance of the reality of matter, and on a separation of the
notion of immortality from its former relations with human personality. Unconsciously they adopted a definition of Paul Janet:
"l'infini, c'est le réel des choses moins la limite."[20] Taking the concrete as the basis of the infinite, they were to try in various ways to
free it of the "limite." If science professed to stop at matter and to
concentrate its efforts on the investigation of the "enchaînement des
phénomènes,"[21] which presupposed order and could be systematized
by reason, the artist sought the spontaneous essence of matter, which
the scientist did not deny but refused to explore.

As I shall try to show in what follows, this new mysticism was
developed in poetry concurrently with the philosophic evolution of
the latter part of the nineteenth and the beginning of the twentieth
centuries; far from being dependent in its later manifestations on
the influences of Bergsonism, it had its own evolution and established its own tradition. But whereas the theories of the philosophers remained in the realm of abstraction, poetry illustrated this
concept of an infinite based on the unconditional acceptance of concrete reality. Not satisfied with asserting the infinite possibilities of
matter, art would attempt to act upon it. If science would dethrone
the metaphysical or speculative infinite, the poet who was learning
to cultivate the power to create was ready to substitute what Renan
called "l'infini réel" and was eager to undertake a new genesis.

20. P. Janet, *op. cit.*, p. 90.
21. P. Janet, "Philosophie et Religion," *Revue des Deux-Mondes*, LXXXI,
p. 349.

I: LAUTRÉAMONT

The most conscious realization, in a poetic work, of this spiritual crisis brought on by scientific progress, is manifested in the brief and violent work of Isidore Ducasse—or Comte de Lautréamont as he chose to call himself—who within the space of a few years lived and mirrored the conflict of the age through which he passed so quickly.

Destined for a scientific career, he arrived in Paris from his native Montevideo as a youth to enter the Ecole Polytechnique. This scientific background is evident in *Les Chants de Maldoror*, not only in his famous invocation of mathematics, but negatively in the resentment and reluctance with which he admits the advances of science within the realm of the occult. This education and its profound effect on a nature that must have started out by being very religious are the bases of the work of one who, after remaining unrecognized for many years, has been claimed by the Surrealists as their foremost precursor.[22]

Lautréamont, though keenly aware of the scientific discoveries of his time, regarded them with great contempt. Why this contempt? Endowed with mystical propensities and an energetic imagination, he would have wished to live in a world that might be putty in his hands; he would have wished a world that he could mold to his own liking and from which he might build unknown but fascinating tributaries leading to heaven. His should have been a world of miracles, of metamorphoses, of revelations. Instead, he had the misfortune of living in an age which was banishing miracles and revelations and supplanting them with unbreakable physical laws; and humanity had not yet reached the stage where it could conciliate physics and metaphysics. Lautréamont found himself in the precarious position of a mystic robbed of his symbols of worship.

The result was twofold. On the one hand he felt a sort of asphyxiation at the thought of man's plight: "qui reste enchaîné à la croûte durcie

22. One Surrealist has said of him: "Sachez . . . que pour moi et pour quelques autres, aucun poète ne *tient* devant Rimbaud, si ce n'est Lautréamont même, qui le dépasse de la tête. Excusez-moi." Open letter of Louis Aragon to Albert Thibaudet, *Nouvelle Revue Française*, 1ᵉʳ avril, 1922, p. 470. Numerous other examples of this sort of admiration could readily be cited.

d'une planète,"[23] at the thought that it was impossible to step outside of physical laws: "Ainsi donc, il est une puissance plus forte que la volonté . . . Malédiction! La pierre voudrait se soustraire aux lois de la pesanteur? Impossible."[24] There was the despair of feeling convinced that there would be nothing beyond the grave: "je sais que mon anéantissement sera complet."[25] On the other hand, there was a stronger reaction: that of revolt, defiance. Man, that stupid animal who thinks he has unveiled the secrets of the universe! In reality, he has not solved the important problems of life: for instance, "le problème effrayant" of "la mortalité ou l'immortalité de l'âme."[26] Gazing upon the latent forces of the ocean, he says: "Il reste à la psychologie beaucoup de progrès à faire. Je te salue, vieil océan."[27] He gloats as he thinks that with all the excellent scientific methods evolved, man has not learned to fathom the abysses of the ocean. "Tu ne laisses pas facilement deviner aux yeux avides des sciences naturelles les mille secrets de ton intime organization; tu es modeste."[28] Modest is the ocean, modest the animals; but man cultivates his knowledge, seeks to elevate himself through it, only to find himself at the end on a level with the animal. No longer would it be possible to draw an illusory picture of the universe, in which the lowest beings that surrounded man would be elevated by the reflected glory of man's love for them. No, even as in science, the poet was beginning to explain the highest forms by the lowest; the characters of Lautréamont easily pass from one form of life to another, and they communicate with each other with the greatest of ease. But would this bond between the creatures of the earth raise matter to the level of the spirit, as Janet had expected? On the contrary, this process was to show "l'homme à la figure de crapaud,"[29] man, directed by the same uncontrolled, illogical instincts as the animal, and in appearance more despicable than the toad. Although we do not reach with the Comte de Lautréamont the glorification of irrationality in man,[30] he nonetheless orients poetry in that direction.

23. Ducasse, (Lautréamont) *Œuvres complètes,* (Agence Centrale de Librairie), p. 122.
24. *Ibid.,* p. 21.
25. *Ibid.,* p. 34.
26. *Ibid.,* p. 42.
27. *Ibid.,* p. 32.
28. *Ibid.,* p. 30.
29. *Ibid.,* p. 49.
30. He had intended his work to be something in the genre of Byron's *Manfred* or Mickiewicz' *Konrad,* "mais cependant bien plus terrible," p. 248.

What he discovers is so distasteful to him that he is seized with an all-consuming hatred of humanity, whose fate is chained to the hardened crust of a planet and to the essence of its perverted soul.[31] "Moi seul contre l'humanité"[32] is his theme. Thus, the same hand that began to uncover the irrational in man introduced a profound anti-social attitude. The symbol of this poetry in prose is a horse, furiously galloping to flee the human eye and enjoy all the examples of the "méchanceté humaine."[33] Lautréamont will show man committing diabolical crimes and gloat over his wickedness. He will have his hero, Maldoror, and his associates attack man physically and make him suffer: ". . . Je suis content de la quantité de mal qu'il te fait, ô race humaine; seulement, je voudrais qu'il t'en fît davantage."[34] He will find revolting the very sight of a human being: "Moi, être assez généreux pour aimer mes semblables. Non, non! Je l'ai résolu depuis le jour de ma naissance. On verra les mondes se détruire, et le granit glisser, comme un cormoran, sur la surface des flots, avant que je touche la main infâme d'un être humain."[35] Maldoror will want to kill a child so that it may never reach the complete repulsiveness of the adult. In truth, man had not sustained such a loss of prestige since the fall of Adam as at the hand of Isidore Ducasse!

It was not enough to hate humanity; under the guise of Maldoror, Lautréamont tried to show himself extrahuman. Maldoror took the forms of various animals and returned with pain to his former shape: "Revenir à ma forme primitive fut pour moi une douleur si grande, que pendant les nuits j'en pleure encore.[36] To feel himself extrahuman Maldoror will have to become a monster: one who can neither weep nor laugh, who ignores love and friendship, in brief: "celui qui a tout renié, père, mère, Providence, amour, idéal."[37]

His revolt will be directed not merely against humanity, but against the Creator as well: "Ma poésie ne consistera qu'à attaquer par tous les moyens, l'homme cette fauve, et le Créateur, qui n'aurait pas dû engendrer une pareille vermine."[38]

Paul Janet had hoped that materialism might mean: thinking of God

31. Ducasse, *op. cit.*, p. 122.
32. *Ibid.*, p. 122.
33. *Ibid.*, p. 35.
34. *Ibid.*, p. 69.
35. *Ibid.*, p. 58.
36. *Ibid.*, p. 139.
37. *Ibid.*, p. 184.
38. *Ibid.*, p. 56.

as belonging *in* the world, and seeing the world in the spirit of God. But the opposite was to happen. Lautréamont did picture the Creator in the world which he had created, but by so doing debased Him rather than raised the things that He touched with His breath. The Creator was to take the form of the rhinoceros, was to behave in foul ways. Previously *good* had been associated with the search for the infinite. But for the monster that was Maldoror right and wrong were no longer to be considered as contradictory. They could be committed simultaneously and were equally directed toward the search for the infinite.[39] If God was in him and in all other creatures, thought Maldoror, He must reside in the very essence of living things; and he had found this essence to be evil rather than good. Thus, the Creator, according to Lautréamont, was a source of evil. When Maldoror sees dogs furiously howling as if in hatred against the stars, the trees, the earth, life and silence, and finally tearing each other to death, he hears his mother say:

> Lorsque tu seras dans ton lit, que tu entendras les aboiements des chiens dans la campagne, cache-toi dans la couverture, ne tourne pas en dérision ce qu'ils font: ils ont soif insatiable de l'infini, comme toi, comme moi, comme le reste des humains, à la figure pâle et longue. Même, je te permets de te mettre devant la fenêtre pour contempler ce spectacle, qui est assez sublime.[40]

He associates his own craving for the infinite with that of these hounds: "Moi, comme les chiens, j'éprouve le besoin de l'infini. Je ne puis, je ne puis, contenter ce besoin! Je suis fils de l'homme et de la femme, d'après ce qu'on m'a dit. Ça m'étonne . . . je croyais être davantage."[41]

But if God refuses to reveal to him the mysteries among which his existence is stifling, even as He refuses it to the animals, he, Maldoror, will find other means of discovering the unlimited field of new uncertain horizons: " . . . Je lui [au Créateur] ferai comprendre qu'il n'est pas le seul maître de l'univers; que plusieurs phénomènes qui relèvent directement d'une connaissance plus approfondie de la nature des choses, déposent en faveur de l'opinion contraire.[42] His concept of the infinite will not be abstract but will rather consist of "le principe

39. See the intermingling of pity and cruelty, p. 24.
40. Ducasse, *op. cit.*, p. 27.
41. *Ibid.*, pp. 27-8.
42. *Ibid.*, p. 192.

spirituel qui préside aux fonctions physiologiques de la chair."[43] With him, therefore, will originate the notion that artistic expression can result from a scientific method of exploration of the thinker's subjectivity.

The one barrier to this free exploration is seen to be the forbidding restrictions proffered by reason: "L'homme et moi," bewails Maldoror, "claquemurés dans les limites de notre intelligence comme souvent un lac dans une ceinture d'îles de corail."[44] The important thing to do, therefore, was to try to decrease the restraining effect of this force upon his "besoin d'infini." He found that intelligence could temporarily be destroyed by the "tourbillon des facultés inconscientes,"[45] by simulating the effects of chloroform and even insanity, by producing a forced drowsiness of the senses. Thus began a scientific experimentation, a veritable human vivisection in literature: "Un assoupissement ineffable enveloppe de ses pavots magiques, comme d'un voile qui tamise la lumière du jour, la puissance active de mes sens et les forces vivaces de mon imagination.[46] Not only reason, but even imagination will be relegated to a secondary role; for since it is based on exterior experience, it is considered not only impotent but misleading. Thus, having muted reason and imagination, he will hope to find an abnormal deviation in the functioning of natural laws, and thus there might be revealed to him phenomena beyond those furnished by observation and experience. Nature can be altered to the point of derision. Maldoror will make no distinction between a donkey eating a fig and a fig eating a donkey. He will readily accept on the same level of vision pillars and pins, a rhinoceros and a fly as proof of: "les contradictions réelles et inexplicables qui habitent les lobes du cerveau humain."[47]

From contempt of experience to a contempt of memory there is but a short step. Unlike the poets before him, whose imagery was so greatly dependent on memory, Lautréamont states: "il n'aura pas tort, celui qui prétendra que je ne possède pas la faculté des souvenirs."[48] To replace memory he mixes the remembrance with the dream, and thence the real and the illusion. For instance at a moment when he has drifted into

43. Ducasse, *op. cit.*, p. 177.
44. *Ibid.*, p. 122.
45. *Ibid.*, p. 102.
46. *Ibid.*, p 63.
47. *Ibid.*, p. 125.
48. *Ibid.*, p. 137.

what appears to be a fantastic description of a fabulous spider he reverses fact and fiction and says: "Nous ne sommes plus dans la narration . . . Hélas! nous sommes maintenant arrivés dans le réel,"[49] whereas Arnim would have tried to conciliate the abnormality of the spider with the logic of what had preceded.

What poetry, or rather what manual for future poetry, results from an "état d'âme" in which reason, imagination, and memory are disregarded? The intermittent blotting out of human faculties throws the spotlight on one sense at a time, dimming all others: magnifies the sensation of touch at a certain moment by a series of images including the slipping of a foot on a frog, the crushing of a fly, the sting of a whip; or suddenly awakes the sense of hearing in one who had been deaf, and by so doing blots out all else for the moment; by its keenness it makes him hear the impossible, such as the brushing of the wings of a mosquito against the air, and by its acuteness it destroys the perfect balance that nature had devised for the five senses.

But above all, Lautréamont creates images that rise and fall, follow each other unlinked, unrelated, though interwound, just as in a nightmare. He willfully develops a technique for the representation of what Baudelaire would have called "le rêve surnaturel." He is not concerned with pretty dreams, but with the nightmare in all its absurdities which the ordinary human being fortunately forgets when he awakes; it is the synthetic nightmare of one who had fought natural sleep; it is a far more authentic representation than that of Gérard de Nerval, who had known natural nightmares but had been loath to give them a place in literature. It is the work of one who with perspicacious logic analyzes his voluntary irrationality after having placed himself in a state wherein he can feel sleep without succumbing to it.

Lautréamont is a comedian, cruel, destructive, impudently young, as many of those following him will be; he is a comedian who plays with his audience as well as with the very foundations of the world. At one moment he will blandly confess "ma raison s'était envolée,"[50] but the next moment he will make it clear that he has said it to mislead us; and he will emphasize his autonomy: "Ma raison ne s'envole jamais comme je le disais pour vous tromper."[51] With almost scientific accu-

49. *Ibid.*, p. 171.
50. *Ibid.*, p. 86.
51. *Ibid.*, p. 87.

racy, however, he can simulate the visions of one whose mind has really fled away; the symptoms he attributes to Maldoror are, for instance, strangely akin to those found by Edmond de Goncourt in the mental disturbance of his brother: loss of memory, dehumanization, childish egoism, loss of sleep.[52] All this is reconstructed synthetically with the natural grain of insanity that is latent in the mind of the poet-comedian, like the natural grain of opium to which Baudelaire gave scope. And he is guided by an ever vigilant will:

> . . . Il m'arrive quelquefois de rêver mais sans perdre un seul instant le vivace sentiment de ma personnalité et la libre faculté de me mouvoir: sachez que le cauchemar qui se cache dans les angles phosphoriques de l'ombre, la fièvre qui palpe mon visage avec son moignon, chaque animal qui dresse sa griffe sanglante, eh bien, c'est ma volonté qui, pour donner un aliment stable à son activité perpétuelle, les fait tourner en rond.[53]

Such is the nightmare of one who had willfully turned himself into a monster in order to shirk "la condition humaine" regulated by nature. The boy who had gazed at the stars in scorn or despair, who had in vain looked within the secretive ocean, who had not been satisfied to walk along the abrupt path of the terrestrial journey, had found his outlet in the unpredictable, uncontrollable irrationality enclosed within the mind's shell of logic.

But his work, though printed, was kept from the public, by a publisher who, as Lautréamont explained in a letter to a family friend, Durasse, in 1870, was afraid that "la vie y était peinte sous des couleurs trop amères"[54] and that it might, therefore, anger the public censor. This fact, and the need for financial aid from his parents, made Lautréamont discover a final method of expression: the use of contradiction. In his letter to Durasse, Lautréamont says that he has decided to change his notion of life, to sing from then on only of hope, calm, happiness, duty, and that he expects to receive his father's financial help by informing him of the completion of the preface of this book of *Poésies*. The preface is all that was ever written. But are we to believe that Lautréamont was suddenly convinced of the greatness of human

52. E. Goncourt, *Journal*, no. 3, see pages 246-252.
53. Ducasse, *op. cit.*, p. 157.
54. *Ibid.*, p. 248.

life, of the wisdom of God, of universal order, of love of family, and respect for social institutions? Was he truly convinced that great thoughts generated from reason, that man was perfect, infallible, modest, kind, a kindred spirit of the angel, and that his friends increased in his unhappiness, that to be great meant *not* to consider oneself "misérable," that nothing was incomprehensible, that nothing had yet been said, that the poet had come too early into the world, that poetry should be created by all and not by one, that criticism of poetry was of greater value than poetry itself, that description of heaven could have nothing in common with the materials of earth, that contradiction was the very mark of falsehood?

Or was it rather by this very contradiction that he wanted to deride humanity for the last time, and show that "l'homme dit hypocritement oui et pense non."[55] Was he then saying one last time: man is imperfect and evil, reason is inadequate, order nonexistent, Elohim[56] is lacking in all wisdom, heaven is found only in matter, poetry is the crystallization of the very subjectivity of one lonely being.

At any rate, this curious appendage to his work—an example of extreme irony—cannot belie the fact that Lautréamont produced the first of a series of forced aberrations that were to manifest themselves in poetry. And as Arthur Rimbaud was saying at that very same time: he who attempts the disorder of the mind mutilates himself. Even so, Lautréamont's creative forces had not only turned to the destruction of the things around him, but they had created a hell where the poet vivisected himself and at the age of twenty-four was destroyed. He died with the hope that one day his theories would be accepted by some literary group. As for his own work, he gave it himself its tragic epitaph: "Libre comme la tempête, il est venu échouer, un jour, sur les plages indomptables de sa terrible volonté."[57]

55. Ducasse, *op. cit.*, p. 32.
56. It is to be noted that in order to mention God he uses the word of the ancient Hebrews to denote a god *foreign* to their concept.
57. Ducasse, *op. cit.*, p. 126.

II: RIMBAUD

At the same time that Lautréamont was mutilating himself in order to break with human nature and seek the unknown, Arthur Rimbaud, a youth in his teens, was making an even more daring attempt to *change life*.

Rimbaud has often been analysed and explained with a detailed documentation. He has been termed, in turn, a realist,[58] spiritualist,[59] catholic,[60] anti-catholic[61] nihilist,[62] rationalist,[63] sensualist,[64] anarchist,[65] communist,[66] and humanitarian.[67] Through this kaleidoscopic character with which Rimbaud has been endowed, one light shines more clearly than all the others: his extreme youth; and it seems to me that it is this aspect of the personality of the poet which has played the most important part in his work, and that can conciliate many of the contradictory characteristics found in his poetry. The aim here is not to dissect further the complexity of Rimbaud, but rather to ascertain the historic position of his poetry in the literary upheaval of which it is a part.

Arthur Rimbaud was a phenomenon, and as such embodied the deviation from nature toward which poetry was being oriented. At heart, the deviation that his poetry represents is akin to the sensations experienced in childhood! Every child in his dreams plays that delightful game of creating a world which is as far removed from this one as possible, a world that becomes more and more absurd as his efforts to pass the limits of the known are increased. Although childhood is a time of deep faith in the reality of religion, its mystical representations are part of its ability to see the concrete world in a different light. This

58. See François Ruchon, *J. A. Rimbaud;* Marcel Coulon, *Le Problème de Rimbaud, poète maudit.*
59. See Daniel-Rops, *Rimbaud, le drame spirituel;* Rolland de Renéville, *Rimbaud le voyant.*
60. See P. Berrichon, *J. A. Rimbaud*; P. Claudel, *Positions et propositions.*
61. See M. Coulon, *op. cit.;* to a lesser extent: Jacques Rivière, *Nouvelle Revue Française,* juillet-août, 1914.
62. See Rolland de Renéville, *op. cit.*
63. See Ernest Delahaye, *Rimbaud.*
64. *Ibid.*
65. See Coulon, *op. cit.;* Humphrey Hare, *Sketch for a Portrait of Rimbaud.*
66. See Y. Etiemble, *Rimbaud.*
67. See Rolland de Renéville, *op. cit.*

has little in common with the abstractions of the adult; rather it has the same concrete basis that we have seen the Surrealists consciously seek out in their concept of the infinite. And one day, the child realizes that imagination has of necessity a basis in exterior reality; then he despairs, he buries his imagination, and knowing it to be a futile attempt, he abandons this type of reverie. That is the story of Rimbaud's life and poetry, it seems to me; only—by a miracle—that imagination of childhood, somewhat prolonged in him, was still his when he prematurely developed the philosophical and verbal power which should have come much later, after that excessively imaginative impluse had been attenuated. Precocious as he was, Rimbaud produced "Le Bateau Ivre," *Les Illuminations*, and *Une Saison en Enfer*, through which he conveyed the only image perhaps ever recorded of the world as seen through children's eyes, a world wholly incompatible with the age of reason.

As is the case with all the works we are here analyzing, a series of rejections forms the basis upon which Rimbaud's poetic world, vivified by childhood imagination and experience, which were natural to him and which he succeeded in putting to artistic use, must stand. He approaches art with the instinct for destruction so common in children: to seek the new he must start with a clear slate. With unmistakable pleasure he discards the past. Like Lautréamont he spurns natural memories: "inspecter l'invisible et entendre l'inouï" does not mean "reprendre l'esprit des choses mortes."[68] He will not abide with the mental restraints imposed by things remembered. He will use memories in a novel way: they will not direct creative impluse as they had done in the past; on the contrary, they will be guided by it, be its humble nourishment.[69] The result will be a series of detached sensations arranged not in logical sequence of time and place, but in such a way as to record "découvertes dont on n'a pas de relations."[70] While Lautréamont expressed a simple disdain of memory, Rimbaud made out of this negation one of his means of breaking with normal human experience and giving rise to pseudo souvenirs.[71] These ersatz memories will find an important place in the technique of the future poet.

However, Rimbaud's instinct for destruction was not only concerned with the dislocating of exterior nature, but even more with a disharmo-

---

68. Letter to M. Demeny, 15 mai 1871 (J. M. Carré, *Lettres de la vie littéraire d'A. Rimbaud*).

69. Rimbaud, *Les Illuminations*, p. 101.

70. Rimbaud, *Une Saison en Enfer*, p. 66.

71. For examples see *Les Illuminations*, "Mémoire," pp. 29-31.

nizing of his "moi." He had said early in his poetry: ". . . l'Homme a fini, l'Homme a joué tous les rôles."[72] The "Démon" that the "vierge folle" describes in *Une Saison en Enfer* has the same extrahuman characteristics as Maldoror: he has tried to break his emotional links with country, society, family, love—which he believed had to be reinvented. He even tried to escape the very happiness which he declared fatally inherent in human nature: "Je vis que tous les êtres ont une fatalité de bonheur."[73] But although he said: "Quant au bonheur, établi, domestique ou non . . . non, je ne peux pas,"[74] nevertheless he found happiness pursuing him: "Le Bonheur était ma fatalité, mon remords, mon ver."[75] In the first version of his little poem "Bonheur" he describes the power of this happiness "que nul n'élude."[76] It takes hold of him the moment that the voice of the cock is heard. What did he mean by "chaque fois que chante le coq gaulois?" In the old folksongs and stories there often occurs the expression: "Le coq chanta; il était jour, et mon conte est fini." The voice of the cock was supposed to dissipate the fantastic, the imaginary, the work of art. In Rimbaud's poem happiness begins its reign with the chant of the cock. Even as the cock, it disperses all the poet's efforts and takes possession of his life, instead of serving as an inspiration as in the case of the Romanticists. In the second version of the poem, appearing in *Une Saison en Enfer,* he adds:

> *L'heure de la fuite, hélas!*
> *Sera l'heure du trépas.*[77]

Although he shirks happiness, he knows that only in death can man rid himself of this earthly experience.

But the greatest reaction of all was against reason. As Rimbaud explained in his famous "Lettre du Voyant," he came to believe that the poet would attain the vision he was seeking only when he had lost its intelligibility: "Il arrive a l'*inconnu;* et quand, affolé, il finirait par perdre l'intelligence de ses visions, il les a vues!"[78]

Like Lautréamont, Rimbaud perceived in the progress of science its irremediable shortcomings: "Ah, la science ne va pas assez vite pour

72. Rimbaud, *Œuvres complètes,* "Soleil et chair," p. 25.
73. Rimbaud, *Une Saison en Enfer,* p. 78.
74. *Ibid.,* "Mauvais Sang," p. 33.
75. *Ibid.,* p. 80.
76. *Ibid.,* p. 49.
77. *Ibid.,* p. 81.
78. Letter to M. Demeny, 15 moi 1871.

nous!"[79] he cried out in *Une Saison en Enfer,* and repeated: "La science est trop lente."[80] If, therefore, reason directed science, which had not yet been able to change life, then the "seer," as the poet wished to think of himself, instead of being a prisoner to his reason, would seek on the contrary, through irrational forces, to lift the veil of exterior reality: ". . . J'écartai du ciel l'azur, qui est du noir, et je vécus, étincelle d'or de la lumière *nature*."[81]

He draws aside the azure, i.e. apparent nature, and finds "la lumière nature," i.e. the first, the original light and vision. Like his contemporary, Rimbaud finds new fields of poetic exploration through the cult of the irrational, and like Lautréamont, tries to simulate insanity in his own person: "Aucun des sophismes de la folie,—la folie qu'on enferme —n'a été oublié par moi: je pourrais les redire tous, je tiens le système."[82] Thus, with Rimbaud, as with Lautréamont, we have the first examples of objective experimentation in vivisectional subjectivity. Rimbaud's work, however, is not a manual in the sense that Lautréamont's can be considered; for the first time the theory is applied fully to the work of art. For this *system* of "dérèglement" of the mind and the senses is not confined to introspection although it originates in a release from exterior reality; on the contrary, it brings him to grips with nature and makes it possible for him to inject his irrationality into it, just like the child who builds the fairy world that his flexible mind can fashion upon the set world of the adult.

His system, as he points out himself, is based on simple hallucination. In order to make nature the object of these hallucinations, he eliminates from it one of its essential characteristics, that of *movement* both in time and space; his expression of release from the known aspects of nature will not be manifested in the traditional desire for physical displacement, but in the opposite ideal of immobility.

"Le Bateau ivre" is the voyage of one who has not moved, since he has more landscapes within himself than most people who have come in contact with the diversities of nature. His knowledge of the world came to him, he says, at the age of twelve in an attic.[83] He prefers a stagnant pool to the widest movements of the oceans:

79. A. Rimbaud, *op. cit.,* p. 90.
80. *Ibid.,* p. 96.
81. *Ibid.,* p. 75.
82. *Ibid.,* p. 79.
83. *Ibid.,* p. 156.

Si je désire une eau d'Europe, c'est la flache
Noire et froide où vers le crépuscule embaumé
Un enfant accroupi, plein de tristesse, lâche
Un bateau frêle comme un papillon de mai.[84]

A voyage is not a revelation of the new but on the contrary a means
of "Distraire les enchantements assemblés sur mon cerveau"[85] as
Rimbaud explains elsewhere. He mocks action, "ce cher point du
monde;"[86] to him action is not life but "une façon de gâcher quelque force, un énervement."[87] The symbol of this physical immobility becomes "mon canot toujours fixe; et sa chaîne tirée."[88] Why
immobility?[89] Immobility means freedom from the limitations of
space: if you are immobile you seek no end; you are thus independent of space. Through this distortion of the concept of movement, Rimbaud is able to confuse time and space. To the *"new*
reason" movement means: "arrivée de toujours tu t'en iras partout."[90]
In breaking away from the limitations of time and space, he can present a vast panorama in which centuries and horizons intermingle in
his visions of cities, scenes, tableaux and have at the same time the
static appearance of tremendous frescoes.

In speaking of Rimbaud, Paul Claudel has justly said: "ce n'est
pas de fuir qu'il s'agit mais de trouver."[91] Everything is to be found,
made over: love, stars, sounds, flowers, language. Only the creative
impulse, i.e. the inner action which manifests itself in a minimum
of outer action, is capable of this feat. Speaking of his new reason,

84. Rimbaud, *Œuvres complètes,* p. 105.
85. Rimbaud, *Une Saison en Enfer,* "Délire II," p. 79.
86. *Ibid.,* "Mauvais Sang," p. 33.
87. *Ibid.,* "Delire II," p. 78.
88. *Ibid.,* "Mauvais Sang," 32.
89. See the development of this concept of immobility in A. Salmon's
Dernières Féeries where voyage takes on an entirely new meaning:

> Je rêve de la gare d'où les trains ne partent plus . . .
> Ne plus voir aux portières s'accrocher le jour blême,
> O ne plus agiter de mouchoirs sur le Rhin!
> N'être plus attendu! n'être plus pèlerin!
> Ne plus partir, enfin, pour partir, quoi, quand même!
> Bah! l'immobilité c'est encore un beau voyage,
> Il faut se résigner et s'asseoir sur les bagages, . . .
>
> *Voyages,* pp. 138-9.

90. Rimbaud, *Les Illuminations,* "A une raison," p. 82.
91. P. Claudel, "Préface aux Œuvres d'A. Rimbaud," *Positions et Propositions,*
I, 138.

Rimbaud says: "Un coup de ton doigt sur le tambour décharge tous les sons et commence la nouvelle harmonie."[92] But in order to give substance to the new harmony and carry it beyond a philosophical concept, a technique is necessary; the basis of this representation is, as Rimbaud states it, the simple hallucination. Where did he find these hallucinations? Not so much in artificial paradises as in something that was much closer to his own nature!

He experienced hallucination in a return to the sensations of childhood which had not yet become alien to him: imagery not restrained by preconceived mental sets. This is not memory but a return to the original sensation, "la lumière nature:" to see nature in what the adult would call an "unnatural" manner, in the way he saw it for the first time, and that most people forget as they pass beyond that initial stage.[93]

For instance, an image such as the following in "Enfance II:" "O les calvaires et les moulins du désert, les îles et les meules"[94] has little meaning in the adult plane of perceptions: each of the objects mentioned has a definite reality, but the link is hard to imagine if the idea that these objects evokes is stronger than the sensation. But for the child there is a great natural link between "calvaire" and "moulin." It is not a reasonable association but a sensory one. "Calvaire" means the cross; taken from the purely sensory point of view, a mill has the same shape as the cross he has seen in the countryside; likewise, a haystack in the middle of a flat field looks like an island in the wide expanse of the sea. To most adults, calvary is a much more emotional and mental reality, far removed from a mill, hence the improbability of the verbal association. Thus, by returning to original childhood sensations, he creates what to the adult logic will seem new, illogical visions, though made of the oldest elements of which he has experience. Again elsewhere, even as unnatural an image as: "une cathédrale qui descend et un lac qui monte"[95] consists of a tiny motion of a hand, which will turn storybook pictures upside down, and this illogical aspect of the image will have as much sensory reality as the previously accepted one.

Many of the marvelous tales of childhood form the basis of his

92. Rimbaud, *Les Illuminations,* p. 81.
93. See development of this theme in chapter "The Road to the Absolute," *infra.*
94. Rimbaud, *op. cit.,* p. 144.
95. *Ibid.,* p. 145.

extraordinary imagery: the immobile, artificial characters with orange lips, in bright satins, are story book pictures remembered and brought to life in new and far more unnatural forms. The prose poem entitled "Enfance" in which children and giants, and jewels and flowers are all placed on the same plane of existence, all given the same type of nature, is the culmination of all these childhood wonders:

> L'essaim des feuilles d'or entoure la maison du général. Ils sont dans le midi.—On suit la route rouge pour arriver à l'auberge vide. Le château est à vendre: les persiennes sont détachées. Le curé aura emporté la clef de l'église. Autour du parc, les loges des gardes sont inhabitées. Les palissades sont si hautes qu'on ne voit que les cimes bruissantes. D'ailleurs, il n'y a rien à voir là-dedans.[96]

How strangely reminiscent of the scene in "La Belle au bois dormant," when the prince discovers the sleeping palace!

In imitation of these fairy tales Rimbaud has created some of his own with the same artificial aspect, far removed from the natural form of things about him, but concrete nevertheless. Here are his new flowers: "D'un gradin d'or—parmi les cordons de soie, les gazes grises, les velours verts et les disques de cristal qui noircissent comme du bronze au soleil—je vois la digitale s'ouvrir sur un tapis de filigranes d'argent, d'yeux et de chevelures"[97] and his new cities: "Du détroit d'indigo aux mers d'Ossian, sur le sable rose et orange qu'a lavé le ciel vineux, viennent de monter et de se croiser des boulevards de cristal habités incontinent par de jeunes familles pauvres qui s'alimentent chez les fruitiers."[98]

But this artificiality in individual forms was not the only element that Rimbaud borrowed from the fairy tale. What must have attracted him to it even more was the fact that the fairy tale had been the only form of art that reconciled the contradictions which even the most imaginative adult mind found to exist between reality and the dream. Based on just such a contradiction is, for example, the following image in "Barbare": "Oh! le pavillon en viande saignante sur la soie des mers et des fleurs arctiques (elles n'existent pas)"[99]

96. *Ibid.*, pp. 143-4.
97. *Ibid.*, "Fleurs," p. 71.
98. *Ibid.*, "Métropolitain," p. 113.
99. *Ibid.*, "Barbare," pp. 64-5.

or the mingling of the living and the dead in: "C'est elle, la petite morte, derrière les rosiers, . . . La jeune maman trépassée descend le perron . . . Le petit frère (il est aux Indes) là, devant le couchant, sur le pré d'œillets . . . les vieux qu'on a enterrés tout droits dans le rempart aux giroflées."[100] As long as the representation of the image is possible, the reality of it is of no significance. Two prose poems "Royauté" and "Conte" are based entirely on this apparent contradiction which a child can accept.

But an even greater source for this system of hallucinations was to be found in the absurdities of popular childhood songs, absurd only to a mellowed reason, but vital and plausible to the virgin vision of a child. When Rimbaud confesses in *Une Saison en Enfer* that: "La vieillerie poétique avait une bonne part dans mon alchimie du verbe,"[101] was he not referring to jingles such as the following which appears to have been popular in the nineteenth century, and particularly in the valley of the Meuse where Rimbaud passed his childhood:

> *Ah! j'ai vu, j'ai vu*
> *—Compère, qu'as-tu vu?*
> *—J'ai vu une vache*
> *Danser sur la glace*
> *En plein coeur d'été*
> *—Compère vous mentez.*
>
> *Ah! j'ai vu etc. . .*
> *—J'ai vu une grenouille*
> *Qui filait sa quenouille*
> *Au bord d'un fossé. . . .*
>
> *—J'ai vu une mouche*
> *Qui se rinçait la bouche*
> *Avec un pavé. . . .*
>
> *—J'ai vu une carpe*
> *Qui pinçait de la harpe*
> *Au haut d'un clocher. . . .*

100. Rimbaud, *op. cit.*, "Enfance," p. 143.
101. Rimbaud, *Une Saison en Enfer*, "Délire II," p. 70.

autre variante
J'ai vu la frontière
Dans une rivière
Sur un reverbère
Jouer du violon.[102]

Here we have the seed of the simple hallucination to which he
claimed to have become accustomed:

> Je m'habituai à l'hallucination simple: je voyais très franche-
> ment une mosquée à la place d'une usine, une école de tambours
> faite par des anges, les calèches sur les routes du ciel, un salon
> au fond d'un lac; les monstres, les mystères: un titre de vaude-
> ville dressait des épouvantes devant moi.[103]

Hallucination had thus become reality to Rimbaud and absurdities
such as he described were *"frankly"* believable to him, as they are to
a child reciting nonsense rimes or reading fairy tales. By accepting
these aberrations, he will find it possible to mingle sensations:
tastes will fly: "un goût de cendre vole dans l'air,"[104] colors will
sing: "il sonne une cloche de feu rose dans les nuages,"[105] flowers
will speak: "Sur les versants, des moissons de fleurs grandes comme
nos armes et nos coupes mugissent,"[106] or "Des fleurs magiques
bourdonnaient."[107] Even as in these childhood rimes, the contradiction will not only appear in the mingling of sensations, but as an
integral part of the language; thus Rimbaud and his successors will
avert the step that many others were to take, leading from fantasy
to pure symbolism, in which the world of the concrete was entirely
to be replaced by that of the symbol. Not so with Rimbaud and all
those who after him developed the concept of surreality! Without

102. Eugène Rolland, *Rimes et jeux de l'enfance,* pp. 107-110. A remarkable
affinity with these nonsense rimes can increasingly be seen in the works of the
precursors of Surrealism. See for example Maeterlinck, *Serres chaudes*:
> J'entends célébrer une fête un dimanche de famine
> Il y a une ambulance au milieu de la moisson. . . .
> Oh! Il doit y avoir quelque part une énorme flotte sur un marais!
> Et je crois que les cygnes ont couvé des corbeaux!
>   "Cloches de Verres," p. 18.
103. Rimbaud, *Une Saison en Enfer,* p. 70.
104. Rimbaud, *Les Illuminations,* "Phrases," p. 92.
105. *Ibid.,* p. 93.
106. Rimbaud, *Ibid.,* "Villes I," p. 107.
107. *Ibid.,* "Enfance," p. 144.

transition, the abstract concept is linked to the concrete entity: "Sur les passerelles de l'abîme et les toits des auberges, l'ardeur du ciel pavoise les mâts,"[108] or "Des accords mineurs se croisent et filent; des cordes montent des berges."[109] The tactual is linked with the remote: "j'ai tendu des cordes de clocher à clocher; des guirlandes de fenêtre à fenêtre; des chaînes d'or d'étoile à étoile, et je danse."[110] It is the childhood impression of authenticity in the fantasy that plays havoc with natural laws and creates a new supernatural in an attempt to say "adieu au monde;"[111] all the while one is kept very much in contact with the material world.

Here, then, is the form that Rimbaud's visions take, based on an anti-rational, anti-emotional attitude and represented through the technique of the most primitive hallucination. This disorder of the mind through which Rimbaud distorted nature but kept within the bounds of materialism came to be considered sacred by him: "Je finis par trouver sacré le désordre de mon esprit."[112] It was to form the very essence of his mysticism. For his revelation of the unheard, unseen, unimaginable, of the infinite, is based neither on Christian belief nor a deistic attitude. His visions of the beyond are neither a philosophical concept nor a theological representation. Eternity was what a child might imagine: "C'est la mer allée avec le soleil;"[113] eternity, lodging in the material world but contradicting its natural laws! Creation linked once more with contradiction and destruction!

And what of his "enfer"? Rimbaud, who said "La morale est la faiblesse de la cervelle"[114] and who demanded "la liberté dans le

---

108. *Ibid.*, "Villes I," p. 107.
109. *Ibid.*, "Ouvriers," p. 135.
110. *Ibid.*, "Phrases," p. 93.
111. Rimbaud, *Une Saison en Enfer*, "Délire II," p. 71.
112. *Ibid.*, p. 71.
113. Rimbaud, *Les Illuminations*, "Eternité," p. 38. The representation of eternity as an irrational sensation will occur often later on. See Tzara: "La Mort de Guillaume Apollinaire:"

> si la neige tombait en haut
> si le soleil montait chez nous pendant la nuit pour nous chauffer
> et les arbres pendaient avec leur consonne—unique pleur—
> si les oiseaux étaient parmi nous pour se mirer
> dans le lac tranquille audessus de nos têtes
>   On Pourrait Comprendre
>   —*De nos oiseaux*, p. 113.

114. Rimbaud, *Une Saison en Enfer*, p. 78.

salut"[115] was not seeking the hell of Christian penitence. His objection to the orthodox conception of hell was that it had nothing new: it had been brought within the range of normal human perception. Christianity was not a means of escaping from the known according to Rimbaud, for everything was foreseen: "c'est encore la vie!"[116] It was even established that hell was below and heaven above![117] If he attempts to picture himself in this theological hell, he is not prompted by any religious feeling; on the contrary he entitled his "Nuit de l'Enfer" in the *Ebauches à une saison en Enfer,* a "Fausse Conversion" to which he is led by an infinite despair that turns him against everything: "la nature, les objets, moi, que je veux déchirer."[118] If he insists that he finds himself in hell, it is because his "Saison en Enfer" might make it possible for him to rend apart himself and everything around him, and by so doing, realize his blasphemous longing to unveil all the mysteries of heaven and earth: "Je vais dévoiler tous les mystères: mystères religieux ou naturels, mort, naissance, avenir, passé, cosmogonie, néant."[119] Plunging into hell while still possessed of life, this would provide him with an human experiment in the process of gradually divesting himself of the limited forms of earthly existence: to reach hell would necessitate the gradual destruction of the man by his own will: time would cease, sound pass, touch vanish . . . . And out of this fire of destruction would dart the sparks of instinct and impulse; to Rimbaud as to Baudelaire and Lautréamont this liberated impulse was to be associated with "le mal:" "O sorcières, ô misères, ô haine, c'est à vous que mon trésor a été confié."[120]

But while the instincts received a rather vague representation in Lautréamont's work, Rimbaud for the first time gave them the form and color of images. For instance, in speaking of "La Faim" and "La Soif" he evoked his ancestors; this suggested the depth of the impulse; at the same time he indicated a hunger for things that one would be incapable of eating; thus one is able to grasp the wide scope and primeval nature of the craving:

115. Rimbaud, *op. cit.,* p. 33.
116. *Ibid.,* "Nuit de l'Enfer," p. 40.
117. *Ibid.,* p. 43.
118. *Œuvres complètes, Ebauches d'une Saison en Enfer,* p. 248.
119. Rimbaud, *Une Saison en Enfer,* p. 43.
120. *Ibid.,* p. 7.

Si j'ai du goût, ce n'est guère
Que pour la terre et les pierres.
Dinn! dinn! dinn! Mangeons l'air,
Le roc, les charbons, le fer.[121]

The same procedure indicating depth and insatiability is used in the representation of the sex instinct, by building the images around the intensity of the initial impulse of a "tout jeune homme" and a chaste seminary novice.[122]

Rimbaud did not envision one single inferno but many "Je devrais avoir mon enfer pour la colère, mon enfer pour l'orgueil,—et l'enfer de la caresse; un concert d'enfers."[123] The poems entitled "Fêtes de la faim" and "Soifs" originally went under the title of "Enfer de la faim" and "Enfer de la soif." Each inferno was the formula for the expression of an experience intensified beyond natural proportions; though it borrowed as little stimulus as possible from exterior reality, it preserved a concrete existence.

Through an alienation of sensations, through penetration of the instincts and repulsion of the organized world of nature and of the *a priori* character of the supernatural, Rimbaud claimed to have become: "un inventeur bien autrement méritant que tous ceux qui m'ont précédé."[124] This personal world that Rimbaud had created and whose key he prided himself as being the only one to possess, was to be the locale of the inner image destined to become at the same time the subject and the object of the seekers of surreality.

But Rimbaud had reached his limit. As he recounts in his autobiographical *Saison en Enfer,* his desire for flight from reality had made him choke human joy, had directed him toward evil and made him skirt the limits of sanity. But at the age when every human being closes forever his eyes on that first vivid image of the world, without having given any artistic or literary representation of it, when the veil descends on the "lumière nature," Rimbaud also realizes that he will never really reach the unimaginable, sees even his "ingénuité physique amèrement rassise,"[125]—when not yet twenty. Despite all his mutilation of self, he knows that "On ne

---

121. Rimbaud, *Les Illuminations,* "Fêtes de la faim," p. 51.
122. See *Œuvres complètes, Déserts de l'amour,* p. 115 and *Un Cœur sous une soutane,* p. 253.
123. Rimbaud, *Une Saison en enfer,* p. 45.
124. Rimbaud, *Les Illuminations,* "Vies," p. 155.
125. *Ibid.,* p. 151.

part pas."[126] He has kept before his eyes the image of the motionless rowboat beyond which lie the flowers that he will never touch
although he may dream of them: "O bras trop courts!"[127]

Finally the despair of resignation takes the place of the hopeful
defiance of adolescence:

> J'ai essayé d'inventer de nouvelles fleurs, de nouveaux astres, de
> nouvelles chairs, de nouvelles langues. J'ai cru acquérir des
> pouvoirs surnaturels. Eh bien! je dois enterrer mon imagina-
> tion et mes souvenirs! Une belle gloire d'artiste et de conteur
> emportée![128]

He who thought himself a "mage," or an angel, exempt from all
morality, is thrown back upon the soil with "a responsibility to
find, and an exacting reality to attain! Peasant!"[129]

From poet to peasant—peasant in the fullest, grimmest sense of
the word. Tied to this earth, part of its very make-up! He returns
to the earthly "festin" from which he had sought in vain to escape.
He tries to learn not to hate life even if he is to be its slave: "Es-
claves, ne maudissons pas la vie."[130] He who had so completely expressed the creative effort of extreme youth was reduced to silence;
and the real voyages that followed his literary silence after 1873
were not escape toward the unattainable. Rather they were a renunciation of magic: "On ne part pas.—Reprenons les chemins
d'ici."[131] But not without having pointed out the hazardous paths
to magic along which those to follow might venture a little farther!

III: MALLARME, AUTHOR OF *IGITUR*

In the poetry of Lautréamont and Rimbaud, a distortion of natural phenomena seemed to take the place of the metaphysical world
repudiated by science. Rimbaud tried to free the idea of the inconceivable from its dependence on death: he pictured the eternal as a

126. Rimbaud, *Une Saison en enfer*, "Mauvais Sang," p. 22.
127. *Les Illuminations*, "Mémoire," p. 32.
128. *Une Saison en enfer*, "Adieu," p. 109.
129. *Ibid.*, p. 109.
130. *Ibid.*, p. 103.
131. *Ibid.*, p. 22.

deviation rather than a harmonious evolution of the natural. But at about the same time, Stephane Mallarmé was considering an even more difficult experiment: that of experiencing death with his human mind and senses.

Between 1867 and 1870, Mallarmé, an obscure and lonely provincial school teacher, conceived what he considered the outlines of his most important work: mirroring his innermost being, whose key he believed he had discovered. But Mallarmé realized that he had moved beyond his age, and as he said looking back in 1885: "j'ai été dix ans d'avance du côté où de jeunes esprits pareils devaient tourner aujourd'hui."[132] Not only did he not dare publish *Igitur*, but he showed it only to two of his closest friends: Catulle Mendès and Villiers de l'Isle-Adam. Mendès carried away from the reading of the work only the regret of not having dared reprimand Mallarmé for having produced such a thing. He sorrowfully attributed this composition to the reclusive life of the poet during his years in the south of France away from his friends, and he lamented that this solitude had drawn his friend into a "fausse voie" which would rob him of his "charm" and "clarity."[133] As for Villiers, he said nothing; but years later his *Axel,* about which he had started to think as early as 1862, seemed to echo the strange magic of which he had caught such a brief glimpse in the work of his friend.[134]

Mallarmé did not publish *Igitur* or the *Folie d'Elbehnon*; and he even added to it the epitaph of "Déchet," waste! It was to be found after his death by Dr. Bonniot, his son-in-law, and published in 1925 in two sections: the work in its last form before Mallarmé abandoned it, and the earlier drafts assembled by Dr. Bonniot under the heading of "Scolies." In referring to the work here, no distinction is made between the two parts as they essentially embody one vision and are equally incomplete representations of the final form of the author's thought. Since *Igitur* was only published in 1925, it may be considered negligible as a direct influence on the poetic de-

---

132. See Mallarmé, *Autobiographie* and *Bibliographie des poètes maudits, I Stephane Mallarmé.*

133. See Catulle Mendès, *Le Mouvement poétique français de 1867-1900* p. 140.

134. Dr. Bonniot, who edited the text, is inclined to think that Villiers de l'Isle-Adam showed in *Axel* the influence of Mallarmé's *Igitur*. On the other hand, Mallarmé might easily have had in mind the personality and appearance of Villiers when he fashioned his *seeker of the absolute.*

velopment of Mallarmé's immediate successors; but from the point of view of literary history it appears even more significant than the works of Lautréamont and Rimbaud. For this strange experience of the sensation of death, attempted in *Igitur*, is the first poetic work based entirely on the materialistic mysticism which later turned out to be the basis of Surrealism and for three generations of poets replaced the concept of immortality by what they thought of as the absolute.

Although in his later work—save his very last, "Un Coup de dés jamais n'abolira le hasard"—Mallarmé dealt with themes less daring and more conforming to human reason, he seems to have remained all his life uncertain as to the significance of the Christian concept of eternity. As far as human life was concerned, he saw within himself two opposing desires for flight: one against "la Chair" and all physical desires and experiences, and the other against the equally violent tendency toward complete abstraction from physical self and toward total identification with the "Azur."[135]

Igitur, undertaking the journey to the tomb, finds a compromise between these two longings for escape. Like Baudelaire's "Voyage," Igitur's is an adventure in the realm of the unknown; but after the initial call to death, Mallarmé pictures in detail Igitur's exploration of the various stages of the descent to the "néant" as he gropes his way through a series of jostles and shocks: first, "Minuit," or the cessation of *time*; then, "l'escalier," i.e. the intermediary steps between the finite and the infinite, "le coup de dés," which represents Igitur's *will* to break irrevocably with life, and "le sommeil sur les cendres"—final communion with the absolute. In seeking to experience with his human senses the transition between life and death, it is not immortality that Igitur wants; the only immortality that he can conceive for the individual is to re-enter into his race, and lose his identity. Heretofore the poet and the philosopher had imagined the infinite as existing in a realm beyond the concrete and beyond the grasp of material senses; their speculations as to eternity had sought to represent the unattainable by material symbols or complete abstractions, but had imagined the final evolution of these forms as lying outside of earthly perceptions and concept. But Mal-

135. Compare "Fenêtres" and "Azur" for this conflict in the escapism of Mallarmé. Villiers poses the same problem in *Axel*.

larmé, having banished the possibility of personal immortality, wants to experience the "néant" here and now; thus, instead of speculating about immortality after death, he will seek the absolute which *denies* immortality: "Puis—comme il aura parlé selon l'absolu —qui nie l'immortalité,—l'absolu existera en dehors—lune au-dessus du temps: et il soulèvera les rideaux, en face."[136] But this absolute, which is independent of the barriers of life and death, is not a spiritualization of reality; rather it is a materialization of the infinite, which is no longer thought to reside outside of the experience of life, but is, on the contrary, to be found within the concrete entities of the world after they have been divested of their external physical nature.

However, Mallarmé found one great barrier to the absolute: this barrier was "le hasard," the force which alone separated existence into created time and uncreated "ténèbres" and thus tended to keep the infinite outside of the reach of the material world. Igitur's life, therefore, is directed toward one single act, symbolized in the blowing out of the candle followed by the casting of the dice: "Lui-même à la fin, quand les bruits auront disparu, tirera une preuve de quelque chose de grand (pas d'astres? le hasard annulé?) de ce simple fait qu'il peut causer l'ombre en soufflant sur la lumière."[137] By concentrating the human will on the performance of this one human act, he believes that he may have abolished "hazard" and in so doing freed the infinite of its control: "L'infini sort du hasard que vous avez nié."[138]

But granted that the absolute is envisaged as a separate entity and not as a subjective perpetuation of perfected human experience after death, how will it be represented by the artist? How will he represent "la substance du néant"?[139] The very expression gives the key to the answer. The existence of the absolute can be asserted only through an acceptance of the absurd. For the difference between the finite world and the infinite is that in the former we recognize the juxtaposition of opposites as "absurd," while the power of "hazard" which nullifies this contradiction in things can be said, *from our point of view,* "to contain the absurd." But the very fact that contradictory forces are reconciled by the greater forces of "hazard," makes Igitur

136. Mallarmé, *Igitur,* p. 36.
137. *Ibid.,* p. 35.
138. *Ibid.,* p. 37.
139. *Ibid.,* p. 51.

believe that the absurd no longer exists. The infinite, therefore, is the plane of reality in which combinations that we might call absurd or impossible are accepted as possible. And "hazard," which turns what we call "absurd" into reality, permits, by that same token, the infinite to exist:

> Bref dans un acte où le hasard est en jeu, c'est toujours le hasard qui accomplit sa propre Idée en s'affirmant ou se niant. Devant son existence la négation et l'affirmation viennent échouer. Il contient l'Absurde—l'implique, mais à l'état latent et l'empêche d'exister: ce qui permet à l'Infini d'être.[140]

Igitur is "un personnage . . . qui sent en lui, grâce à l'absurde, l'existence de l'Absolu."[141] The contradictions to which Rimbaud resorted are here exaggerated to the point where they represent the absurd, which will henceforth become the basis of artistic creation and a means of liberating art from the finite and the natural aspects of things and beings for the seekers of the absolute.

To arrive at this new "conscience de soi," based on the absurd, Igitur must, to an even greater extent than Maldoror, disintegrate his human make-up and isolate himself from humanity,[142] give up emotion and reason, forget the human word, separate the self that thinks and feels from the self that undergoes the experience: "Tombeaux-cendres, (pas sentiment, ni esprit) neutralité!"[143]

Not only will Igitur lose natural characteristics, but so will inanimate objects lose their natural attributes without being dissolved into abstractions:

> . . . Il s'est refait, voyant la glace horriblement nulle, s'y voyant entouré d'une raréfaction, absence d'atmosphère, et les meubles tordre leurs chimères dans le vide, et les rideaux frissonner invisiblement, inquiets: alors il ouvre les meubles pour qu'ils versent leur mystère, l'inconnu, leur mémoire, leur silence, facultés et impressions humaines,—et quand il croit être redevenu lui, il fixe de son âme l'horloge, dont l'heure disparaît par la glace, ou va s'enfouir dans les rideaux.[144]

140. Mallarmé, *op. cit.*, p. 60.
141. *Ibid.*, p. 62.
142. *Ibid.*, p. 60.
143. *Ibid.*, p. 37.
144. *Ibid.*, pp. 55-7.

The room expires, leaving Igitur with a horrible sensation of eternity.[144] He sees one by one the objects around him slowly dying:

> . . . Projetant leurs lignes dures dans l'absence d'atmosphère, les monstres figés dans leur effort dernier, et que les rideaux cessant d'être inquiets tombassent, avec une attitude qu'ils devaient conserver à jamais.[144]

What will be the state of physical phenomena in the realm of the absolute? A vacuum will replace atmosphere; sound will be robbed of all its characteristics except the *beat:* "le battement seul reste;"[145] as a result we are to envisage the abnormal sensation of rhythm without sound: "un double heurt, qui n'atteint plus ou pas encore sa notion, et dont un frôlement actuel, tel qu'il doit avoir lieu, remplit confusément l'équivoque, ou sa cessation."[146] Light will likewise be divested of everything but its shadow; it will consist of what remains after the candle has been blown out: shadow and its reflection: "pour que l'ombre dernier se mirât en son propre soi."[147] Perception of these shadowy aspects, based as it is on the absurd, will grasp such unnatural spectacles as "une vision de panneaux à la fois ouverts et fermés."[148] Barriers between the visual and the auditory need no longer exist in this world of "battement" and "ombre":

> . . . L'étendue de couches d'ombre, rendue à la nuit pure, de toutes ses nuits pareilles apparues, des couches à jamais séparées d'elles et que sans doute elles ne connurent pas—qui n'est, je le sais, que le prolongement absurde du bruit de la fermeture de la porte sépulcrale dont l'entrée de ce puits rappelle la porte.[149]

Thus, in this extraordinary image, seeing is represented as the ultimate manifestation of hearing.

Like Baudelaire, Mallarmé is very conscious of the restrictions of "time." Igitur says: "J'ai toujours vécu mon âme fixée sur l'hor-

---

145. *Ibid.,* p. 43.
146. *Ibid.,* pp. 43-4.
147. *Ibid.,* p. 45.
148. *Ibid.,* p. 77.
149. *Ibid.,* p. 46.

loge."[150] Time, as we know it, will vanish therefore, and be replaced by "Minuit absolu" which is conceived as:

> . . . Le rêve pur d'un Minuit, en soi disparu, et dont la clarté reconnue, qui seule demeure au sein de son accomplissement, plongé dans l'ombre, résume sa stérilité sur la pâleur d'un livre ouvert que présente la table.[151]

In this new concept, the past and the future are identical since "time" no longer divides them.

As for space, it loses its significance since movement is virtually eliminated; the only movements still remaining are: "le mouvement suspendu" of the pendulum with its uncertain "double heurt impossible" swinging from the possible to the impossible.[152] Or else he records infinitesimal motions such as: "l'unique frisson était le travail arachnéen d'une dentelle qui retombait sur le velours."[153] Otherwise everything that claims existence in the absolute must try to free itself of movement,[154] and adopt a "vertigineuse immobilité."[155] Here we have the same attempt at destruction of movement as noticed in Rimbaud's work, but on a far larger scale. Motion, which used to be the symbol of escape in the romantic tradition, is henceforth to be considered the antithesis of the absolute, and later the antithesis of the surreal as André Breton explains in his definition of "convulsive beauty:"

> The word that I have used in the title of this short essay to qualify the only kind of beauty that should be served in our time, would lose its whole meaning for me if it were imagined as being in movement instead of in the exact expiration of this movement. In my opinion, there can be no beauty—convulsive beauty—except at the price of the affirmation of the reciprocal relationship that joins an object in movement to the same object in repose.[156]

150. *Ibid.*, p. 53.
151. *Ibid.*, pp. 40-1.
152. *Ibid.*, p. 77.
153. *Ibid.*, p. 72.
154. *Ibid.*, p. 68.
155. *Ibid.*, p. 70.
156. A. Breton, *What Is Surrealism?*, p. 39. This article does not appear in the French version of the 'brochure' entitled "Qu'est-ce que le Surréalisme?"

Thus, the disintegration of nature creates the absolute: light, color, sound, time, and finally movement disappear, leaving objects in a state of void, and awaiting, even as a painting of the Surrealist Yves Tanguy, a new world of music and light, instead of evoking forgotten sensations of the past. And Igitur who enters into the absolute by descending "les escaliers de l'esprit humain"[157] finds himself in this overflowing emptiness, pulsing silence and shining darkness, as a man blind and deaf and dumb, and freed of personal misery and happiness. For even as the objects that he had known all his life have shed all the trivialities of exterior reality in order to assume their eternal attitudes, and even as the hour has fled forever from the clock, so Igitur's superficial human attributes have also vanished to such an extent that his image has disappeared from the mirror—or been absorbed. . . . Here we have the same state as is described in the commentary of Piet Mondrian's "Picture" which appeared in N. Y. during World War II in a Surrealist exhibition, entitled: *Artists in Exile:*

> Only what is pure and above personal happiness and personal misery is balanced and unchangeable. Art achieves this equilibrium by substituting [for] the individual and [for] the apparent, the pure relationship of the universal to be found both in our unconscious self and in the outer world. By means of composition the individual will be abolished.

By entering within the race, by means of the "corridors oubliés depuis l'enfance,"[158] Igitur loses his personality and abolishes the individual just as the later Surrealists were to do. Thus, the most extreme manifestations of the will of the individual to transcend nature result in the abolition of the individual, and the supreme effort of the mind in the breakdown of its logical make-up. Insanity underlies the voyage of Igitur; for he who sought the absolute and separated himself from the rest of humanity, he who ventured into the disorder of a world in conflict with the forces of "le hasard:" "a oublié la parole humaine en le grimoire et la pensée en un luminaire."[159]

157. Mallarmé, *op. cit.,* p. 37.
158. *Ibid.,* p. 79.
159. *Ibid.,* p. 62.

IN THE spiritual crisis, exemplified in poetry by the work of these three contemporaries, Lautréamont, Rimbaud, and Mallarmé, the following basic characteristics marked a change in the mysticism of the artist.

1. A tendency to disregard the natural phenomenon and to refuse to imitate it in art: by divesting it of the concepts of time, space, and movement.

2. A tendency toward dehumanization through a detachment from human emotions as evidenced in a rejection of human happiness and the acquisition of antisocial tendencies; and a rejection of certain mental processes: reasonable perceptions, memory.

3. A change in the notion of eternity, freeing this concept from that of personal immortality: regarding eternity as a distortion rather than an evolution or perfection of natural entities, searching for it in matter rather than considering the absolute as the antithesis of matter.

In these works are the beginnings of the technique that might reveal this other reality attributed to matter, i.e. the acceptance of the absurd as a means of artistic expression.

CHAPTER V

The Road to the Absolute

Ceux qui sont une source de mépris
Ceux qui portent en eux la goutte d'eternité
nécessaire à la vie
Ceux qui n'ont jamais connu leur mesure
En passant sur la route qui n'est recouverte que par le
ciel baissant la tête
Des étoïles sont restées prises dans leurs cheveux
—Reverdy

THE POETRY of Rimbaud, Lautréamont, and Mallarmé was a deliberate step toward creation through a conscious process of destruction, toward nihilism through extreme individualism. After 1870, the destructive force related to the search for the absolute seemed to have worn itself out, and it was the creative side of the balance that was to carry the greater weight until the outbreak of Dadaism.

After the initial "balayage" of outer reality, poetry did not long remain satisfied with the voluntary silence of Rimbaud, the abstinence of Mallarmé or the apology of Lautréamont. The will to represent and to convey—without which art is but abstraction—asserted itself and sought to crystallize the new mysticism in a technique that would renovate traditional themes by giving substance to the concept of an infinite existing in matter. This road to the Absolute was to be taken by succeeding generations of poets.

Included in this chapter will be poets from 1885 to the early 1920's. Among those classified as a rule as Symbolists we shall deal with the following: Jules Laforgue, traveller, cosmic visionary, and disillusioned, melancholy Dane, dead at twenty-seven; Maeterlinck, —not the author of philosophic treatises—but the young author of a small volume of poems, entitled *Serres chaudes*, in which the exterior world is transfigured by a covering of glass; Saint-Pol-Roux, long relegated to a secondary rank, not as striking a figure as some of the other Symbolists, but a technician, the "M. Teste" of the visionaries, whose patient, lucid efforts bridged from one century to the next and left the best source book of the theories and techniques that his fellow poets put into practice. At the turn of the century is Gide, the twenty-eight year old poet of *Les Nourritures terrestres,* which was to influence so many of the young men of the pre-war period; we are not dealing with the famed author who in 1927 apologized for having written "ce livre de jeunesse,"[1] but rather with a Gide exhilarated by his own powers, wanting to change his life by coming to grips with nature, and feeling strong enough to deal with it. In the early years of the century there is Apollinaire, the new blood, earthy, yet mystical, vulgar at times, crying louder than anyone since Baudelaire: "du nouveau," and attempting to raise his head above those who were not aware that a new century had begun. Finally, we come to Pierre Reverdy and Jules Supervielle, working on the margin of Dadaism and Surrealism, feeling with them new realities, assimilating the new technique, profiting from the disintegration of old artistic laws in order to find new vistas and new themes, but making the new freedom theirs discreetly. . . . These and a few others[2] sought the Road to the Absolute. Their works reflect the development of a new poetic mysticism and its effects on the art of writing.

The mysticism that spent its first "élan" of energy in revolt against the accepted forms of nature and their representation, continued to react against the physical limits of the world, and the abstract, remote notion of another world. It is only necessary to call to witness the cosmic longing of Jules Laforgue:

> Notre père qui êtes aux cieux (*oh! là-haut*
> *Infini qui êtes donc si inconcevable!*)
> Donnez-nous notre pain quotidien . . . *Oh! plutôt,*
> *Laissez-nous nous asseoir un peu à Votre Table! . . .* [3]

His dissatisfaction with existing mysticism:

> *Et que Dieu n'est-il pas à refaire?*[4]

1. André Gide, Préface à l'Edition de 1927, *Œuvres complètes,* II, 228.
2. A number of other poets might also have been included in the present study. In order to keep within reasonable bounds I have tried to illustrate my points by referring to selections that are not only representative of the authors cited, but also of others who might as fittingly have been quoted.
3. Jules Laforgue, "Petite Prière sans prétention," *Œuvres complètes,* I², 36.
4. *Ibid.,* I¹, 247.

and elsewhere:

> *O culte d'un Dieu qui n'est pas,*
> *Quand feras-tu taire tes cloches!*[5]

and his profound defeatist materialism which makes him conclude:

> *. . . ainsi pour moi*
> *Qui crois qu'ici-bas tout finit au cimetière*[6]

THE SYMBOL

But gradually the revelation of the presence of the infinite in matter is considered a subjective act of exploration rather than a denial of the limitations of objective reality: the dominant symbol of this exploration is the familiar one of the voyage, but a voyage totally transformed. Whereas a voyage was considered by the Romanticists a means of enlarging space and populating time, a means of releasing physical energy and increasing exterior stimuli, the voyage that will now be evolved will seek, on the contrary, to limit and concentrate time and space to the minimum, divest it as much as possible of physical movement, free the explorer little by little from exterior stimuli and horizons, and surround the traveller with such landscapes as will reveal a changed relationship in regard to nature. This voyage was to represent the poet's orientation toward his inner absolute image of exterior entities: "descendre l'escalier humain," as Mallarmé had termed it; "une descente en Moi"[7] in Laforgue's words, "marcher les yeux en dedans" as Saint-Pol-Roux later defined it.[8]

The initial disgust with the traditional voyage had been evidenced in Baudelaire's "Voyage,"[9] which spurned forever the banal account of the "parcoureurs du monde" and their glorification of exterior reality. In place of the ordinary voyage he had imagined a new one:

5. *Ibid.*, "Complaintes des crépuscules célibataires," I², 103.
6. *Ibid.*, "Excuse macabre," p. 203.
7. *Ibid.*, "Ballade," I², 58.
8. Saint-Pol-Roux, *Les Reposoirs de la procession*, I, 117.
9. See *supra*, Chapter III, pp. 50-1.

"Nous voulons voyager sans vapeur et sans voile!"[10] As we noticed, Rimbaud and Mallarmé attacked the finite attributes of movement. Voyage had meant to Rimbaud a child's boat, floating almost motionless in a stagnant pond. Henceforth, a long series of variations of this new symbol of voyage will occur:[11] no sails, no oars, a phantom ship, so independent of exterior reality that it needs no one to steer it and nothing to guide it through its multitudinous visions:

> . . . *je rechois en enfance*
> *Mon bateau de fleurs est prêt. . .*[12]
> > —Laforgue

> *Las, la nef sans pilote ni cordages*
> *S'en ira sombrer vers les horizons*
> *et les pèlerins ne sauront pas l'orage,*
> > *l'orage de nos destins.*[13]
> > > —Kahn

> *L'Océan occupé par de plus beaux navires*
> *Comme par des lys des pelouses et comme par des oiseaux*
> *Laissera s'égarer au courant de ses eaux*
> *Notre nacelle chavirée.*[14]

> > —Gide

Gide's "nacelle" is Alfred Jarry's "nef," which is pictured gliding on immobile waters without the aid of sails or oars:

> *Nef*
> *dont l'avant tombe à pic et bref,*
> *abats tes mâts, tes voiles, noires trames,*
> *glisse sur les flots marcescents*
> > *sans*
> > *rames*[15]

10. Baudelaire, *Les Fleurs du mal*, "Voyage," p. 232.
11. In all these variations the influence of Baudelaire can be clearly seen.
12. Laforgue, *op. cit.*, I', 269.
13. Gustave Kahn, *Premiers Poèmes*, p. 221.
14. André Gide, *Les Cahiers d'André Walter*, "Poème," *O. C.*, I, p. 258.
15. Alfred Jarry, *Les Minutes de sable mémorial*, p. 58.

And later:

> *Il regarda longtemps les rives qui moururent*
> *Seuls des bateaux d'enfant tremblaient à l'horizon*
> *Un petit bouquet flottant à l'aventure*
> *Couvrit l'océan d'une immense floraison*[16]
> —Apollinaire

> *Est-ce une barque qui traverse*
> *Sans rameur un lac endormi*[17]
> —Supervielle

The immobility of the inner action is contrasted by Saint-Pol-Roux with the futile motion of the explorers of exterior reality:

> . . . "L'action intérieure, voici l'action première, unique; le reste n'est qu'agitation superficielle ou, . . . action seconde. . . . La majorité peut aller des kilomètres, élever des arcs, construire des cités, sans avoir pour cela pratiqué un geste essentiel, absolu, personnel. . . .[18]

Compared to the immobility of man, inanimate forms can almost be thought of as endowed with motion:

> Et même leur fausse mobilité empêche-t-elle la plupart de distinguer l'énergie intérieure qui dirige le monde. Au surplus l'homme est inerte à ce point que, en comparaison de lui, les choses d'aspect immobile se meuvent—telles ces Montagnes dont la marche reste inaperçue.[19]

In *Les Nourritures terrestres*, André Gide, the incessant traveller, whose life was composed of kaleidoscopic changes of milieu, sees in mobility the force that tends to rob human beings of the vision of the absolute forms of reality, by constantly metamorphosing these absolute forms to fit transitory beings, and thereby causing thought to be as ephemeral as sensation. The conclusion to be drawn, therefore, is:

16. Guillaume Apollinaire, "L'Emigrant de Landor Road," *Alcools*, p. 102; see also "Onirocritique," *Il y a*, p. 242.
17. Jules Supervielle, *Gravitations*, p. 93.
18. Saint-Pol-Roux, *op. cit.*, I, 231-2.
19. *Ibid.*, p. 232.

Toute forme ne prend que pour bien peu d'instants le même
être; à travers chacun, elle continue, puis le laisse. Mon âme!
ne t'attache à aucune pensée. Jette chaque pensée au vent du
large qui te l'enlève; tu ne la porteras jamais toi-même jusqu'aux
cieux.

Mobilité des flots, c'est vous qui fîtes si chancelante ma
pensée! Tu ne bâtiras rien sur la vague. Elle s'échappe sous
chaque poids.

Le doux port viendra-t-il, après ces décourageantes dérives,
ces errements de-ci, de-là? où mon âme enfin reposée, sur une
solide jetée près du phare tournant, regardera la mer?[20]

The negation of movement, or its almost ludicrous reduction,
takes many forms in the poetry of the twentieth century. For instance, in Apollinaire's "Brasier," the poet's grandiose vision, pro-
jected beyond earth's atmosphere, is experienced in the immobility
of an armchair seat. In Supervielle's little poem entitled ironically
"Mouvement," one imperceptible movement of a horse's neck makes
the animal embrace the cosmic vision of evolutionary existence, and
makes the poet grasp the infinite power that links this concentrated
movement with that of others, centuries apart.[21]

Finally, since exploration is not to be considered dependent on
movement, and direction is confused, there is no horizon to use as
a measuring rod, the walls of perception draw back, and the image
sheds its frame. As Pierre Reverdy puts it, the voyage takes place in
a "paysage sans cadre."[22]

In this symbol of a voyage repudiating movement, of which we
find an unbroken chain of examples from the time of Rimbaud to
the poetry of 1920, and which retains a uniform character over and
above the various schools of poetry to which its authors may be
said to belong, we can see developing the predominant characteristic of Surrealism: a gradually increasing desire to free matter of
limit, which, as noted in the initial chapter of this study, is the

20. Gide, *Les Nourritures terrestres, O.C.*, II, 106-7. See also *Voyage d'Urien*,
an appropriate title for the new voyage.

21. Supervielle, *op. cit.*, p. 47. See also Reverdy, "Exotisme," "P. O. Midi,"
"La Réalité immobile," in *Les Epaves du ciel*. Compare with similar manifestations: Salmon, *Dernières Féeries*, p. 138-9; Desnos, "André Breton ou Face à
l'infini," *Littérature*, no. 13, p. 13.

22. Pierre Reverdy, *Les Epaves du ciel*, p. 51.

basis of the Surrealist search for a new mysticism. The concept of movement could only exist if the concept of limit were accepted. For if there are no limits, there are no goals, and, therefore, there is no necessity for movement, which always tends toward a goal. The repudiation of movement, therefore, is the first symptom of a far more daring repudiation: that of limit. This refusal to submit artistic creation to the concept of limit, i.e. the scale of measurement used by photography, Guillaume Apollinaire was the first to call "sur-real" in 1918 in his preface to *Les Mamelles de Tirésias,* where he explained that this work represented his determination *not* to limit himself to any one aspect of nature and justified on the basis of this motive his "usage raisonnable des invraisemblances"[23] and his refusal to pay heed to time and place: "j'ai pensé qu'il fallait revenir à la nature même, mais sans l'imiter à la manière des photographies."[24]

THE IMAGE

"Qui suis la flûte dont je joue"

—Apollinaire

Through this method of exploration, what is the image that the poet possesses? He has eliminated the possibility of an imitation of nature by discarding the methods of perceiving its multitudinous variations. As Saint-Pol-Roux states in the preface of his third volume of *Les Reposoirs de la procession*: "La vérité dans l'art ne peut donc être la simple fidélité à laquelle se borne ce qu'on appelle l'imitation de la nature."[25] There is nothing imitative about the "explorateur de l'Absolu,"[26] his work will be a "Naissance" and not a "Renaissance:"[27] "Il ne s'agit plus d'évolution, il va s'agir de convertir la substance connue . . . en une substance imprévue, extraordinaire, et, conséquemment, de transporter la tradition, hors de ses siècles d'oisive habitude, sur la voie laborieuse de l'infini."[28]

23. Guillaume Apollinaire, *Les Mamelles de Tirésias,* p. 36.
24. *Ibid.,* p. 12.
25. Saint-Pol-Roux, *op. cit.,* III, 11.
26. *Ibid.,* "Poésia," p. 258.
27. Saint-Pol-Roux, "Réponse périe en mer," *Mercure de France,* juin, 1913, CIII, 656 (footnote).
28. *Ibid.,* p. 656.

No imitation, no revival, but creation: why say *again*, not *say?* Why do *again*, not *do?* Why *copy* and not *create?* Such is the question that the poet asks himself.[29] Why let his senses, dependent on exterior stimuli, be the only informants of the nervous system? Gide, discussing this question in *Les Cahiers d'André Walter*, would give more freedom to the poet's power of creation: "Il suffit que les centres nerveux soient ébranlés; ce ne sont plus seulement les sens qui les ébranlent alors, la perception extérieure,—mais bien l'intime volonté qui, par eux, crée l'image."[30] Indeed, creation gradually becomes identified with poetry. According to Apollinaire, it is this power alone which can henceforth distinguish the poet from other men; this is how he defines the poet in an article written for the *Mercure de France* in 1918, entitled "L'Esprit nouveau:"

> C'est que poésie et création ne sont qu'une chose; on ne doit appeler poète que celui qui invente, celui qui crée dans la mesure où l'homme peut créer. Le poète est celui qui découvre de nouvelles joies, fussent-elles pénibles à supporter. On peut être poète dans tous les domaines: il suffit que l'on soit aventureux et que l'on aille à la découverte.[31]

Even as God, the poet will want to create in his own image; or to go back to the symbol of the voyage, the characteristics of the landscape, or object perceived, reflect the characteristics of the instrument of voyage: or in more general terms, an identification of the subject with the object occurs. As Gide said in *Les Nourritures:*

> . . . C'est une route à élire dans un pays de toutes parts inconnu, où chacun fait *sa* découverte et, remarque le bien, ne la fait que pour soi, de sorte que la plus incertaine trace dans la plus ignorée Afrique est moins douteuse encore. . . . Mais plutôt les sources seront où les feront couler nos désirs, car le pays n'existe qu'à mesure que le forme notre approche.[32]

The same idea is expressed even more vividly in Saint-Pol-Roux'

29. Saint-Pol-Roux, *op. cit.*, III, 262.

30. Gide, *Les Cahiers d'André Walter*, O.C., I, 142. See *infra*, "Road to Chaos," note 25, for influence of André Gide on the writers of the first generation of the twentieth century.

31. Apollinaire, *Mercure de France*, 1ᵉʳ décembre 1918, p. 392.

32. Gide, *Les Nourritures terrestres*, O.C., II, 62. The underlining is the author's.

description of his subjective voyage and the founding of new countries built through the geometry of the Absolute:

> Géomètre dans l'absolu, l'art va maintenant fonder des pays, pays participant par l'unique souvenir de base à l'univers traditionnel, pays en quelque sorte cadastré d'un paraphe d'auteur; et ces pays originaux où l'heure sera marquée par les battements de coeur du poète, où la vapeur sera faite de son haleine, où les tempêtes et les printemps seront ses joies et ses peines à lui, où l'atmosphère résultera de son fluide, où les ondes exprimeront son émotion, où les forces seront les muscles de son énergie et des énergies subjuguées, ces pays, dis-je, le poète, dans un pathétique enfantement, les meublera de la population spontanée de ses types personnels.[33]

And Apollinaire in his prophecy of the poetry of the future gives to reality a subjective existence rather than an objective one:

> *Nous voulons vous donner de vastes et d'étranges domaines*
> *Où le mystère en fleurs s'offre à qui veut le cueillir*
> *Il y a là des feux nouveaux des couleurs jamais vues*
> *Mille phantasmes impondérables*
> *Auxquels il faut donner de la réalité*[34]

a. *Dehumanization*

If we now look at the poems of voyage from the objective point of view, we shall find in the image the same characteristics as in the instrument. Just as the instrument of the voyage is a phantom ship, detached from the human element, so the image perceived is divested of human and physical limitations.

The substance of Laforgue's image is most often the moon, which is represented as an entity uncontrolled by reason; for reason in Laforgue's eyes is: "Lèpre originelle, ivresse insensée."[35] The moon is envisioned as the symbol of freedom from the temporal:

---

33. Saint-Pol-Roux, "Réponse périe en mer," *Mercure de France*, CIII, 656-7.
34. Apollinaire, "La Jolie Rousse," *Calligrammes*, p. 220. The underlining is mine.
35. Jules Laforgue, *Complaintes*, O.C., I¹, 68.

> *Etre actuel, est-ce du moins*
> *Etre adéquat à quelque chose? . . .*
> *—J'aime mieux*
> *Donc m'en aller selon la Lune.*[36]

The image of a land "sans lendemains[37] is devoid of the last echo of the human voice as recognized in the temporal sphere;[38] it has no trace of human history, emotion nor desire, the land which he reaches by means of the raft of nihilism:

> *Au delà des cris choisis des époques*
> *Au delà des sens, des larmes, des vierges*[39]

The image of the infinite is conceived as a combination of "Léthé" and "Lotos," as the reconciliation of two contradictory notions: loss of human sensation and the magical enjoyment of it:

> *Hotel garni*
> *De l'infini. . . .*
> *Léthé, Lotos*
> *Exaudi nos!*[40]

Though this star (i.e. the moon) is overcome by blindness and has a fossilized atmosphere, one of its rays is enough to rid the poet of the limitations of human life:

> *Astre atteint de cécité, fatal phare*
> *Des vols migrateurs des plaintifs Icarus. . . .*
> *Astre lavé par d'inouis déluges,*
> *Qu'un de tes chastes rayons fébrifuges*
> *Ce soir, pour inonder mes draps, dévie*
> *Que je m'y lave les mains de la vie!*[41]

It is in the sterility of this star that the poet finds his image of a new reality:

36. *Ibid., L'Imitation de notre dame la lune*, p. 249.
37. *Ibid.*, p. 250.
38. *Ibid.*, p. 212.
39. *Ibid.*, p. 212.
40. Laforgue, "Litanies des derniers quartiers de la lune, *O.C.*, I¹, p. 273.
41. *Ibid.*, "Clair de lune," p. 213-4.

> *Et rien ne fait de l'ombre, et ne se désagrège;*
> *Ne naît, ni ne mûrit; . . .*
> *Et pourtant, ah! c'est là qu' on en revient encore*
> *Et toujours, quand on a compris le Madrépore.*[42]

Sometimes this dehumanization takes the form of either a human or cosmic primitivism. If the human element gives the image order and harnesses certain sensations to definite mental restrictions, then the more primitive forms of human reaction to matter would be less limited. There is a good example of this in Alfred Jarry's *Les Minutes de sable mémorial,* wherein the poet represents the initial development of each of the five senses within the fœtus.

This dehumanization or primitivism can be traced in a considerable number of works from the end of the nineteenth century to the 1920's. In *Les Cahiers d'André Walter* André Gide, believing that time and space exist only for man's reason, places the image outside of these limits and wants to free it from the humanizing documentation with which reason and the resources of memory clothe it.[43] The images of his voyage are placed outside of the reach of the seasons, and in "undue" hours. No human beings people these images: just detached, unrelated entities such as the sound of a bugle whose vibration rises in the stillness, a dead sun loath to set as if the earth had stopped moving, crows eternally audible, deer whose leaping had been arrested, and the travellers who, gazing on this landscape, understood that "il ne fallait plus bouger."[44]

The same depopulation, lack of location, cessation of movement of the earth and even of the stars can be felt in Apollinaire's "Brasier," where his boat of exploration is surrounded by flames separating his images from any contact with normal perceptions, or in Jules Supervielle's "Loin de l'humaine saison:"

> *Camarades de fortune,*
> *O figurants de la route,*
> *Savez-vous où nous allons*
> *Loin de l'humaine saison*
> *Derrière un enfant qui joue*
> *A tirer du coeur de l'homme*
> *Ciel et terre, nuit et jour.*[45]

---

42. *Ibid.,* "Climat, faune et flore de la lune," p. 218.
43. Gide, *Les Cahiers d'André Walter, O. C.,* I, 149.
44. *Ibid.,* pp. 184-198.
45. Jules Supervielle, *Gravitations,* p. 158. See also in same collection: "Planètes," "Equipages," "Réveil." Also, *Voyages en soi.*

In the cosmic primitivism of Supervielle's "Matins du monde" we envisage the first, unlimited manifestations of sound:

> *Alentour naissaient mille bruits*
> *Mais si pleins encor de silence*
> *Que l'oreille croyait ouïr*
> *Le chant de sa propre innocence.*[46]

or the waves of the ocean at a time when they had not yet chosen their coastlines, which would later close in on them, and human desires, faculties, parts of the bodies of men and animals, not yet restricted by the eventual synthesis of human and animal life, and free perceptions not yet fixed upon any retina:

> *O regards, serez-vous enfin*
> *Retenues par une rétine*[47]

Or else, we witness the disintegration of the human element through the contemplation of the end of the world and of human synthesis. Typical of this is Pierre Reverdy's "Son de Cloche" wherein he represents the final cessation of life and of movement:

> *Tout s'est éteint*
> *Le vent passe en chantant*
> *Et les arbres frissonnent*
> *Les animaux sont morts*
> *Il n'y a plus personne*
> *Regarde*
> *Les étoiles ont cessé de briller*
> *La terre ne tourne plus*
> *Une tête s'est inclinée*
> *Les cheveux balayant la nuit*
> *Le dernier clocher resté debout*
> *Sonne la nuit*[48]

---

46. *Ibid.*, p. 41.
47. *Ibid.*, "Commencements," p. 44; cf. "Age des cavernes," p. 171.
48. Pierre Reverdy, *Les Epaves du ciel*, p. 99. See also in same collection: "Nomade," p. 122, "La Réalité immobile," pp. 52-3. Cf. Supervielle, *Gravitations:* "Départ," "Le Village sur les flots," "Prophétie," and "La Belle au bois dormant."

b. *The marriage of the concrete and the abstract*

Dehumanization was but an initial step in the process of creating a new image; those who stopped there achieved no more than a rarefaction of the image and revealed a certain inability to construct.[49]

After freeing the concrete from its limits, the next step was to associate it on an equal plane with the abstract, and no longer to consider it as its antithesis. The colonization of the infinite[50] meant the establishment of a ratio between the dehumanization of concrete forms and the humanization of abstract concepts. As Saint-Pol-Roux expressed it, the real meaning of the identification of the subjective with the objective was: "l'art parfait où, par un voisinage étrange, semble presque se spiritualiser la matière et se matérialiser l'idée."[51] When the Absolute which the poet senses extinguishes the visibility of concrete reality, by the same token and to the same degree it crystallizes the abstract and unites the two elements into a single reality. Thus, when Saint-Pol-Roux asks himself whether he is seeing "des cygnes invisibles ou bien des âmes visibles presque,"[52] he is not using a clever turn of speech, nor is he playing with words; this image represents for him the experience of an all encompassing reality. More explicitly, this is how he defines the "sculpture de l'Absolu:"

> Ainsi, moyennant la transcription de la substance par le miroir du monde, tel infini parvient à se définir en du fini, l'abstraction daignant se formuler par des linéaments, se préciser par un squelette, se presque idéoplasticiser: linéaments, squelette, argile dont l'hypothèse est dans mes sens et la réalité dans ma foi.[53]

This mingling of the concrete and the abstract was in itself no

---

49. This can readily be seen in the passages quoted from Laforgue; it is true, it seems to me, of most of the Symbolists.

50. Saint-Pol-Roux, *Les Reposoirs de la procession*, III, 261.

51. Saint-Pol-Roux, "Autour de la conférence de Camille Mauclair sur Maurice Maeterlinck, *Mercure de France*, juin 1892, p. 157.

52. Saint-Pol-Roux, "Les Reliefs," *Mercure de France*, janvier 1891, p. 32 cf. Reverdy's ratio between "les corps légers" and "les esprits lourds," *Les Epaves du ciel*, p. 70.

53. Saint-Pol-Roux, "le Mystère du vent" *Les Reposoirs de la procession*, I, 113-4.

new procedure; instances of it could be found in Romantic poetry, particularly in Victor Hugo's verse. Later it became a very common technique with the majority of the Symbolists, who left innumerable images such as:

> *sur mon âme tu t'accoudas et regardas. . . .*

> *Mon fils bercera ses enfances*
> *Sur la soie de mon rêve vivant*
> —Kahn[54]

> *La Nuit pénible a veillé jusqu'à l'aube*
> *Et le silence est venu vers moi*
> *Reposer son angoisse aux plis de ma robe*
> *Douce de soie en fleurs et fraîche d'émeraudes*
> *Aux feuillages tissés autour du coeur des roses*
> *Le silence a pleuré de voir auprès de moi*
> *La face de la Nuit pâle et morte dans l'aube.*[55]
> —Régnier

> *Les chiens jaunes de mes péchés,*
> *Les hyènes louches de mes haines,*
> *Et sur l'ennui pâle des plaines*
> *Les lions de l'amour couchés!*[56]
> —Maeterlinck

But although the Symbolists all took the same inward direction[57] toward the exploration of a new image, the result in the case of most of them was that the associations between the concrete and the abstract were so logical and followed such an orderly construction that the abstract merely became the symbol of the concrete, and a new reality was not suggested. The images gathered in the limitless landscapes that they sensed were clothed with the very limitations they were trying to forestall.

On the other hand, one of the more successful treatments given this technique in the poetry of the "fin de siècle" can be seen in

---

54. Gustave Kahn, *Les Palais nomades, Premiers poèmes,* pp. 209, 327.
55. Henri de Régnier, *Poèmes,* p. 143.
56. Maurice Maeterlinck, *Serres chaudes,* p. 35.
57. For emphasis of this characteristic in Symbolism see article of Tancrède de Visan on *Maurice Maeterlinck, Vers et Prose,* VIII, 82.

Alfred Jarry's "La Régularité de la châsse"; here the poet in a "gondole spectre" travelling at the same time through sensuous landscapes presented by the physical aspects of the church where he finds himself, and the abstractions arising from religious concepts, combines the two experiences into a single image built with words that fit both realities and serve as a bridge between them:

> Pris
> *dans l'eau calme le granit gris*
> *nous voguons sur la lagune dolente*
> *notre gondole et ses feux d'or*
> *dort*
> *lente.*

> Dais
> *d'un ciel de cendre finlandais*
> *où vont se perdant loin les mornes berges,*
> *n'obscurcis plus, blêmes fanaux,*
> *nos cierges.*

> Nef
> *dont l'avant tombe à pic et bref,*
> *abats tes mâts, tes voiles, noires trames;*
> *glisse sur les flots marcescents*
> *sans rames.*

> Puis
> *dans l'air froid comme un fond de puits*
> *l'orgue nous berçant ouate sa fanfare.*
> *Le vitrail nous montre, écusson,*
> *son*
> *phare.*

> Clair
> *un vol d'esprits flotte dans l'air:*
> *corps aériens transparents, blancs linges,*
> *inquiétants regards dardés*
> *de*
> *sphinges.*

Et
le criblant d'un jeu de palet,
fins disques, brillez au toit gris des limbes
mornes et des souvenirs feus,
bleus
nimbes . . .

La
gondole spectre que hâla
la mort sous les ponts de pierre en ogive,
illuminant son bord brodé
dé
rive.

Mis
tout droits dans le fond, endormis,
nous levons nos yeux morts aux architraves,
d'où les cloches nous versent leurs
pleurs
graves.[58]

An even more striking manifestation of this technique is revealed in Saint-Pol-Roux' prose poem, "Le Fol" where he describes an encounter with an insane person who has escaped from his cell. As he observes the "Fol" who seems to be able to give substance to the "néant," and to possess his dream as if it were visible, the poet wonders whether this mental set could, if cultivated by the normal mind, one day succeed in making even God "saisissable." Enviable is the lot of this inmate for he perhaps already touches God in the same way as he seems to touch the concrete image of the invisible dog that his mind has created:

Cet homme avait une telle façon de saisir certain petit rien de néant et d'en caresser de doigts délicats la plastique absente que ce petit rien ce ne pouvait être qu'une statuette de Tanagra.

Dès le seuil il s'était penché si charmantement pour flatter d'une tape familière une abstraction capricieuse à hauteur de ses genoux que je n'avais pas hésité à penser: 'là est le chien de la maison !' . . .

58. Jarry, *Les Minutes de sable mémorial,* p. 58.

On errait en pleine métaphysique. . . .

. . . Croire posséder son rêve, ne serait-ce pas la suprême fortune? . . . Le monde visible, qu'est-ce en vérité? de l'invisible à la longue solidifié par l'appétit humain. Un jour Dieu sera-t-il traduit en saisissable par la somme des voeux des multitudes,— et d'ailleurs cet homme le touche-t-il déjà, peut-être?[59]

It is the "fol" who best knew how to combine the visible with the invisible; the poet would have to imitate him in order to create this same type of image. He would have to place his work "loin de la falaise logique" of his life.[60] This meant the acceptance of the absurd in the composition of the image; by accepting the absurd the poet would be able to give much more freedom to words, bring about a veritable "Emancipation du Verbe," a new flexibility: ". . . Les premiers mots ornés d'ailes, ailes rendant ces mots susceptibles de bondir de la réalité dans la métaphysique, de la féerie dans le domaine des choses."[61]

There is a prose poem of Saint-Pol-Roux which in its very title bears this contradiction: "L'Ame saisissable." In it the poet attempts to show how transcendence becomes possible to "les Simples"; it is not at a shrine that he discovers them searching the infinite but on the stage set by a buffoon; it is the absurd spectacle that has:

L'estampe finie de l'infini, la géométrie visible de l'invisible, la pantomime perceptible du mystère, la divulgation des hiéroglyphes, la démonstration présumable ou suggestive des théorèmes rebelles à leurs malingres cervelles, autrement dit le spectacle à prix facile des difficultés à acquérir la dive Thulé du rêve inopinément mise à la merci du profane, l'impossible entrevu, l'au-delà cadastré, l'absolu monétisé.[62]

It is absurd painting that reveals to them the possibility of breaking the rules of the finite world: a painting built upon contradictions:

59. Saint-Pol-Roux, *op. cit.*, I, 237-43.
60. *Ibid.*, III, "L'Enfer familial," p. 181. Surrealists tend to give a greater importance to Saint-Pol-Roux than to the majority of the Symbolists; cf. Breton's dedication of *Clair de Terre* (1923): "Au grand poète Saint-Pol-Roux."
61. Saint-Pol-Roux, *op. cit.*, II, 63.
62. *Ibid.*, III, 131 another variation of the same work adds: "l'absolu dévisagé, au-delà concret" *Mercure de France*, IV, 38.

Au fond, à gauche, à droite du haut sol de planches que fouleront les Bizarres bariolés . . . une toile enfantinement peinte s'éploie sur laquelle: une princesse Naine épousant un Roi Géant; un Explorateur en houppelande bleu barbeau, et sous le bras un jaune parapluie, engoulé par un crocodile couleur d'herbe tendre; un Peau-Rouge, qui se débat dans la colique abominable d'un reptile aux écailles d'huitres, et autres parodies d'épouvante.[63]

However, it is not until we reach Apollinaire that we find complete works whose imagery is based on this mystical contradiction of the laws of nature and language. In "L'Enchanteur pourrissant," published in 1921, the word "enchanteur," which in general is wont to evoke the image of the constant renewal of life and the transformation of natural phenomena, is coupled with the word "pourrissant:" the enchanter is dying although immortal; he is breathing within his corpse; in a reversal of the experience of Igitur who, though alive, was able to sense the infinite with his finite senses, the enchanter, though dead, persists, because of his infinite senses, in the finite world in which he no longer holds any other existence but that of putrefaction:

L'enchanteur était entré conscient dans la tombe et s'y était couché comme sont couchés les cadavres. La dame du lac avait laissé retomber la pierre, et voyant le sépulcre clos pour toujours, avait éclaté de rire. L'enchanteur mourut alors. Mais comme il était immortel de nature et que sa mort provenait des incarnations de la dame, il resta vivant en son cadavre.[64]

His vision of the world, therefore, and of all the beings that come to contemplate him, will henceforth convey the same combination of finite and infinite that are present within him. He becomes the "Irréalité raisonnable"[65] around whom are endowed with an identical destiny fictitious and real characters, immortal and mortal entities, the cries of real creatures and the "vols irréels"[66] that pass above his tomb. In this world of the "enchanteur pourrissant" con-

63. Saint-Pol-Roux, *op. cit.* III, 129-30.
64. Apollinaire, *L'Enchanteur pourrissant*, p. 11.
65. *Ibid.*, p. 38.
66. *Ibid.*, p. 14.

traditions such as the following are, therefore, thoroughly acceptable:

the clarity of shadow:

> La Violée: Je ne sais plus rien, tout est ineffable, il n'y a plus d'ombre[67]

the inaudibility of a piercing cry:

> Or, l'enchanteur mort avait tout entendu et comme il détestait les troupeaux, les peuplades et toute congrégation en général, il eut une violente colère et cria et sa voix fut inouïe dans la forêt florale et ensoleillée.[68]

copulation under the dictatorship of the sterile giant Behemoth:

> Les bêtes n'entendirent pas la voix de l'enchanteur et continuèrent leurs copulations mortuaires sous la dictature inféconde de Béhémoth.[68]

the symbol of this fertile sterility, putrefraction, which represents the creativeness of destruction:

> son cadavre était plein de vie.[69]

the flight of the immovable:

> Béhémoth disparut sur place sans cesser d'être immobile.[70]

Some of the contradictions are not only mental but form an intrinsic contradiction in language:

> L'Enchanteur: Hélas! Il y a trop longtemps que vous n'êtes
>   pas immortels.
> Apollonius de Tyane: Le silence rend immortel.
> L'Enchanteur: Tais-toi, silencieux![71]

Apollinaire uses this technique of contradiction in many of his poems. In "Cortège," describing the inverted flight of a bird, he directs its wings upward toward the earth, from the sky's darkness

67. Apollinaire, *L'Enchanteur pourrissant*, p. 42.
68. *Ibid.*, p.56.
69. *Ibid.*, p. 58.
70. *Ibid.*, p. 59.
71. *Ibid.*, p. 75.

to earth's brilliance, and finally sees it dazzled by a light linked neither to heaven nor to earth:

Oiseau tranquille au vol inverse oiseau
Qui nidifie en l'air
A la limite où notre sol brille déjà
Baisse ta deuxième paupière la terre t'éblouit
Quand tu lèves la tête. . . .

Oiseau tranquille au vol inverse oiseau
Qui nidifie en l'air
A la limite où brille déjà ma mémoire
Baisse ta deuxième paupière
Ni à cause du soleil ni à cause de la terre
Mais pour ce feu oblong dont l'intensité ira s'augmentant
Au point qu'il deviendra un jour l'unique lumière[72]

Innumerable examples of the same technique could be cited in other works of this period, which, like Apollinaire's must be distinguished from the exaggerations of Dadaism. In Pierre Reverdy's *Les Epaves du ciel*, the imagery is constantly giving an impression of walls pushing back, doors and windows opening wide only to be confronted with things and beings that immobilize themselves in the face of the freedom that this expansion of space suggests. Objects seem to force nature to act in contradiction to its expected movements: a series of images emitting sudden unexpected visions record in quick succession a lamp that will not be lighted, a bell that will not ring, a sound that will be heard dying, a person that will stop sleeping when night comes, a sun that is heard sweetly ringing.[73]

Finally, if the absurd and the illogical are accepted as integral elements of the image, they can also be accepted as the basis of the relationship between one image and the next. Juxtaposition of irreconcilable entities, composed themselves of contradictory characteristics: that is the basis of the "new reality" of which Guillaume Apollinaire gives previews in "Collines" with pictorial concreteness.

72. Apollinaire, *Alcools*, pp. 54-5.
73. Such images are abundant in Supervielle's *Gravitations*.

Il neige et je brûle et je tremble
Un arbre élancé que balance
Le vent dont les cheveux s'envolent

Un chapeau haut de forme est sur
Une table chargée de fruits,
Les gants sont morts près d'une pomme
Une dame se tord le cou
Auprès d'un monsieur qui s'avale[74]

This technique was to be applied to the most difficult manifestations of all poetic mysticism: that of envisaging the relationship between life and death. Particularly successful examples of this are evident in Apollinaire's "La Maison des morts" and Supervielle's "Le Miroir des morts."

In "La Maison des morts" the poet first presents the irrevocable state of death: bodies lying side by side in their glass cells. Suddenly:

Le ciel se peupla d'une apocalypse
Vivace
Et la terre plate à l'infini
Comme avant Galilée
Se couvrit de mille mythologies immobiles[75]

An angel breaks the glass and there is sudden intercourse between life and death; it becomes impossible to distinguish the living from the dead as they intermingle in a pastoral scene; love is perceived in a new perspective wherein it is closer to death than to life:

Je vous attendrai
Dix ans vingt ans s'il le faut
Votre volonté sera la mienne

Je vous attendrai
Toute votre vie
Répondait la morte[76]

Songs are sung by the living *or* the dead; and the language which Apollinaire has found most flexible as an instrument of communica-

74. Apollinaire, *Calligrammes*, p. 28.
75. Apollinaire, *Alcools*, p. 44.
76. *Ibid.*, pp. 46-7.

tion between the children of this world or of the other is composed
of the absurd words of the old childhood rounds, considered by
him to be the most ancient monuments of poetry. He is undoubtedly
referring to the same type of nonsense rimes which can be linked to
Rimbaud's "hallucinations." Once again it is the *absurd* that pro-
vides a link between material and mystical existence:

> *Des enfants*
> *De ce monde ou bien de l'autre*
> *Chantaient de ces rondes*
> *Aux paroles absurdes et lyriques*
> *Qui sans doute sont les restes*
> *Des plus anciens monuments poétiques*
> *De l'humanité*[77]

As the dead and the living proceed on their journey in close com-
radeship, the ring that the living person had put on the finger of
the dead as a preparation for the complete union to come, breaks
suddenly, emphasizing through this exterior break the inner, in-
alienable unity that the poet is attempting to convey.

Finally the dead re-enter within their tombs but leave the living
in a state of illumination,—shining as if by the light of genius.[78]
Taken in a broader sense, the spark of genius can be said to have
touched the poet and made him independent of all other human
beings only when he has attained the power of associating the mystical with the material, and of envisaging not two existences—one
of life, and the other of death—but, on the contrary, one reality
combining the two experiences:

> *Car y a-t-il rien qui vous élève*
> *Comme d'avoir aimé un mort ou une morte*
> *On devient si pur qu'on en arrive*
> *Dans les glaciers de la mémoire*
> *A se confondre avec le souvenir*
> *On est fortifié pour la vie*
> *Et l'on n'a plus besoin de personne*[79]

77. *Ibid.*, p. 47.
78. *Ibid.*, p. 52.
79. *Ibid.*, p. 52. This is the same life in death that the Scorpions are shown
seeking in *L'Enchanteur pourrissant*, p. 55.

The same type of materio-mystical experience is attempted by Jules Supervielle in *Gravitations*. In "Le Portrait" the poet tries to establish a relationship between himself and his dead mother which will take him outside of life and her outside of death: somewhere between the two stages the outward contradiction between the two existences will become acceptable and identify itself with reality:

> *Nous nous en allons pourtant,*
> *ton portrait avec moi-même,*
> *Si condamnés l'un à l'autre*
> *Que notre pas est semblable*
> *Dans ce pays clandestin*
> *Où nul ne passe que nous.*[80]

What are the obstacles that he has had to face before feeling this contact with the dead? Immobility and silence! He asks the dead to teach him immobility, for it is in movement that he finds the most potent barrier between the finite and the infinite:

> *Aide-moi à être immobile*
> *Tant de gestes nous séparent,*
> *tant de lévriers cruels!*[81]

And just as immobility becomes a positive concept rather than the mere absence of motion, so does silence acquire a concrete but unlimited existence which the poet must dominate in order to overcome the barrier between life and death:

> *. . . . Dominer le silence assourdissant*
> *Qui voudrait nous séparer, nous les morts et les vivants.*[82]

A series of material representations of the mystical experience of death are seen in the collection of poems grouped as: "Le Miroir des morts." In "Les Yeux de la morte" he presents a dead woman whom he knows;" it is not the verb "connaître" that he uses, but the verb "savoir" not used when speaking of human beings; but here the one word "sais" immediately conveys the impression that the poet is expressing a much deeper sense of "knowing:" not su-

---

80. Supervielle, *Gravitations*, p. 14.
81. *Ibid.*, p. 13.
82. *Ibid.*, p. 14.

perficial acquaintance but complete knowledge. The poet does not know the dead as he knows the living; he makes us sense by the unexpected use of this one word that his experience in the field of the absolute has a much deeper meaning than that of the relative world of the living. Then, proceeding to the physical description of "la morte" he uses ordinary terminology in such a manner as to suggest the element of the absurd associated with the absolute.

> *Elle lisse ses cheveux*
> *Et ne sait pas si ses yeux*
> *Vont se fermer ou s'ouvrir.*[83]

In the expectation of a simple act—that of opening or closing of eyes—we are confronted with an image supposing an inconceivable state, similar to that of Mallarmé's open *and* closed panels in Igitur's journey toward death.

The transition between life and death is suggested even more successfully in the little poem "Pointe de flamme." Here again the experience of death is reduced to sensation, or rather clothed with the positive power of an absence of sensation:

> *Tout le long de sa vie*
> *Il avait aimé à lire*
> *Avec une bougie*
> *Et souvent il passait*
> *La main dessus la flamme*
> *Pour se persuader*
> *Qu'il vivait,*
> *Qu'il vivait.*
>
> *Depuis le jour de sa mort*
> *Il tient à côté de lui*
> *Une bougie allumée*
> *Mais garde les mains cachées.*[84]

The foregoing examples seem to reveal the beginning of the new færie which the Surrealists were to seek; it is different from the fantasy of the past which created the fairy tale either by dehumanizing or dematerializing the concrete, or by humanizing or materializing

---

83. Supervielle, *Gravitations*, p. 120.
84. *Ibid.*, p. 124. See also; "la Belle Morte," "La Revenante."

the unsubstantial. Here on the contrary is initiated a fantasy that owes its possibility to the impossibility of convergence of the two states, and its logic to the illogic that creates it.

c. *The cult of the future*

The third element significant in the creation of the new imagery, the element vivifying the new structure, was the faculty of prophecy to be developed through an orientation toward the future.

When the image had been dependent for its substance on exterior documentation, it was memory that had played the most active role in fashioning it; but from the minimizing of exterior data resulted a gradual repudiation of memory and a growing tendency to attenuate its power over the image. The quality of remembering had become associated with that very process of logical reasoning which impeded the perception of the absolute. As André Gide stated: "la mémoire d'autrefois s'en est allée avec la raison morte."[85] In *Les Nourritures terrestres* Gide confided to "Nathanaël" that he had undergone a complete loss of the faculty of recollection:

> Je cherche parfois dans le passé quelque groupe de souvenirs, pour m'en former enfin une histoire, mais je m'y méconnais, et ma vie en déborde. Il me semble ne vivre aussitôt que dans un toujours neuf instant. Ce que l'on appelle: se recueillir m'est une contrainte impossible.[86]

At the same time we find him preaching to Nathanaël the art of forgetting as a means of drawing from the world of matter, sensation and instinct their everlasting newness: "Nathanaël, ne cherche pas dans l'avenir, à retrouver jamais le passé. Saisis de chaque instant la nouveauté irressemblable."[87] Later, in Apollinaire's eyes, the power of remembrance becomes a weak, fragile, passing thing:

> Les souvenirs sont cors de chasse
> Dont meurt le bruit parmi le vent.[88]

---

85. Gide, *Les Cahiers d'André Walter*, O.C., I, 149.
86. Gide, *Les Nourritures terrestres*, O.C., II, 209.
87. *Ibid.*, p. 84.
88. Apollinaire, "Cors de Chasse," *Alcools*, p. 160.

He, too, accords a greater importance to forgetting:

> *Quels sont les grands oublieurs*
> *Qui donc saura nous faire oublier*
> *telle ou telle partie du monde*
> *Où est le Christophe Colomb*
> *à qui l'on devra l'oubli d'un continent?*[89]

But forgetting is not to be considered synonymous with destroying; loss is regarded a necessary step toward greater discovery:

> *Perdre*
> *Mais perdre vraiment*
> *Pour laisser place à la trouvaille*[90]

In ridding himself of the substantial power of remembering, the poet is seeking to acquire the potential power of prediction. According to Rimbaud one of the poet's chief attributes was his ability to be a "voyant." The poets that followed him on the Road to the Absolute tried to cultivate this very power in themselves. When Saint-Pol-Roux saw human victory as a partial colonization of the unknown, this in turn meant to him "de l'avenir ramené au présent:" "L'art ne consiste pas seulement à voir et à sentir son heure, mais principalement à prévoir et à pressentir par delà les limites de son temps les idées impratiquées."[91] The new mysticism that attempted to free art from as many limitations as possible would be obstructed if the poet sought to contemplate his visions with the eye of the past rather than that of the future: "Le mal vient de ce que nous regardons ces éclairs avec l'œil du passé, non celui de l'avenir."[92] The past was synonymous with limit and logic, while the future was limitless, flexible in its formlessness, governed not by logic but by the laws of chance, of "le hasard." Its overwhelming potency fascinated the poet: "Ah! porter en soi-même un seul culte, un seul dieu, l'avenir."[93]

This cult of the future and the element of prophecy which it con-

89. Apollinaire, "Toujours," *Calligrammes,* pp. 110-1.

90. *Ibid.,* p. 111.

91. Saint-Pol-Roux, *Les Reposoirs de la procession,* III, 262.

92. Saint-Pol-Roux, "La Mobilisation de l'imagination," *Mercure de France,* CXX, 225.

93. Charles Cros, "Les Poèmes, ce sont des plaintes," *Mercure de France,* LIII, 60.

tained, was one of the essential characteristics of "l'esprit nouveau" as defined by Apollinaire in 1918:

> L'Esprit nouveau exige qu'on se donne de ces tâches prophétiques. C'est pourquoi vous trouverez trace de prophétie dans la plupart des ouvrages conçus d'après l'esprit nouveau. Les yeux divins de la vie et de l'imagination donnent carrière à une activité poétique toute nouvelle.[94]

Thus the poet knocked at a door never yet opened and challenged the "cavale ardente"[95] of phophecy:

> *Ouvrez-moi cette porte où je frappe en pleurant*
> *La vie est variable aussi bien que l'Euripe*
>
> *Tu regardais un banc de nuages descendre*
> *Avec le paquebot orphelin vers les fièvres futures.*[96]

By daring to envisage the formidable, horizonless sphere of the future, in whose shadow the entire past history of the human race was reduced to ridiculous restrictions, the poet felt in himself the divine power of creation and of magic:

> *Tu vois que flambe l'avenir*
> *Sache que je parle aujourd'hui*
> *Pour annoncer au monde entier*
> *Qu'enfin est né l'art de prédire*
>
> *Certains hommes sont des collines*
> *Qui s'élèvent d'entre les hommes*
> *Et voient au loin tout l'avenir. . . .*
>
> *Profondeurs de la conscience*
> *On vous explorera demain*
> *Et qui sait quels êtres vivants*
> *Seront tirés de ces abîmes*
> *Avec des univers entiers*
>
> *Voici s'élever des prophètes*
> *Comme au loin des collines bleues. . . .*

---

94. Apollinaire, "L'Esprit nouveau," *Mercure de France*, 1ᵉʳ décembre 1918, p. 394.
95. *Ibid.*, p. 396.
96. Apollinaire, "Le Voyageur," *Alcools*, p. 59.

> *On cherchera dans l'homme même*
> *Beaucoup plus qu'on n'y a cherché*
> *On scrutera sa volonté*
> *Et quelle force naîtra d'elle*
> *Sans machine et sans instrument. . . .*
>
> *Jeunesse adieu voici le temps*
> *Où l'on connaîtra l'avenir*
> *Sans mourir de sa connaissance. . . .*
>
> *L'homme se divinisera*
> *Plus pur plus vif et plus savant. . . .*[97]

Tremendous vistas were being opened to the poet; through the contemplation of the future he sensed not only the possibility of exploring the still undiscovered regions of human consciousness but even a complete metamorphosis of human nature and the rebirth of enchanters; that is the prophetic color of *L'Enchanteur pourrissant:* "De longtemps, la terre ne portera plus d'enchanteur, mais les temps des enchanteurs reviendront."[98]

Most of the poems of Apollinaire in which the cult of the future is predominant were written during World War I. At a time of world chaos, which caused such a tremendous schism between the present moment and the past, memory seemed to become subservient to things forever irrevocable, and the present was undesirable, unwanted. The future held not only a significant outlet for *poetic* energy, but there was mingled in this artistic creativeness a certain political optimism. There appeared almost an identification at times of artistic and political victory in the hope of new discoveries not only in art but in human living; such is the twofold meaning and prophecy of Apollinaire's "Victoire:"

> *La Victoire avant tout sera*
> *De bien voir au loin*
> *De tout voir*
> *De près*
> *Et que tout ait un nom nouveau*[99]

97. Apollinaire, "Les Collines," *Calligrammes,* pp. 20-25.
98. Apollinaire, *L'Enchanteur pourrissant,* p. 21.
99. Apollinaire, "La Victoire," *Calligrammes,* p. 218.

Creation, then, implied not only destruction of known forms—such as the tendency toward dehumanization indicated—not only a new relationship between the concrete and the abstract, based on the acceptance of the absurd, but also a degree of speculation and prediction that was to become inherent in the representation of the image. As Apollinaire stated in "L'Esprit nouveau," the new spirit in literature, and particularly in poetry, neither combatted nor identified itself with any one artistic coterie but touched them all to various degrees.

The underlying motive that manifested itself in the characteristics noted in certain of the poetic works of the end of the nineteenth century and early twentieth was an attempt to reach the vision of the Absolute through a new conception of what mysticism might mean. I have here tried to point out only the initial milestones of an evolution that has remained in movement concurrently with the revolutionary aspect of Surrealism. In the chapter to follow it will be observed in what way excesses developed from the general structure of this mysticism: excesses which led a certain group of poets from the Road to the Absolute to the Road to Chaos.

CHAPTER VI

The Road to Chaos

Dada n'était pas un commencement mais une fin
—Benjamin Péret

AGAINST the poet's long, ever more concentrated effort to sense the concrete presence of the absolute, and to fashion a technique that might express the Promethean dream, could be heard a sigh of disillusionment: "Rien!" In the face of every creative "élan" displayed by the poet, there was an inner realization of having accomplished nothing, of having surmounted none of the formidable obstacles in the way of the absolute.

Satiated with exterior reality, Mallarmé had said: "La Chair est triste, hélas, et j'ai lu tous les livres," and Rimbaud: "Assez vu . . . assez eu . . . assez connu. . . ." This disgust with much experienced sensations had become increasingly intense. In Charles Cros' words:

> *J'ai tout touché: le feu, les femmes, et les pommes;*
> *J'ai tout senti: l'hiver, le printemps, et l'été*
> *J'ai tout trouvé, nul mur ne m'ayant arrêté.*[1]

The same feeling had made Apollinaire wish to lay aside all natural things:

> *Je me suis enfin détaché*
> *De toutes choses naturelles*
> *Je peux mourir mais non pécher*
> *Et ce qu'on n'a jamais touché*
> *Je l'ai touché je l'ai palpé*
> *Et j'ai scruté tout ce que nul*
> *Ne peut en rien imaginer*[2]

1. Charles Cros, "Sonnet," *Anthologie KRA,* p. 55.
2. Guillaume Apollinaire, "Les Collines," *Calligrammes,* p. 23.

This detachment had made it possible for poetry to put aside, with cold awareness, the Romanticist's cult of emotionalism; the seekers of the absolute had been trying to accustom themselves to do away with the human concept of happiness, to approach even the phenomenon of death coldly, objectively, and to find in it illumination rather than emotion. In short, they had gradually brought about an abolishment of the "I" by treating it as the object rather than as the subject of their creativeness; as Gide had expressed it in connection with the emotion of grief: "se regarder en souffrir sans penser que c'est soi qui souffre."[3]

But with all this outward sophistication and quasi-scientific objectivism they had not been able to destroy one of the most fundamental and universal of human sensibilities, the inherent despair that Pascal associated with the earthly condition of the "roseau pensant." At first the expression of this despair had taken the form of passive melancholy: the silence of Rimbaud, the apology of Lautréamont. With Jules Laforgue it became a constant obsession which stood between his cosmic visions and his enjoyment of them. In characterizing his fellowmen in a little poem, aptly called "Médiocrité," he summarized his notion of the "Sanglot de la Terre" by the word "Rien:" "Rien, ils n'auront rien su."[4] This same despair is the final note to be heard in Maurice Maeterlinck's *Serres chaudes:* it is the symbol of a hand that marks the obstacle to emancipation:

> *J'étais parfois le plongeur*
> *qui ne peut plus s'évader de l'eau chaude*
> *J'étais parfois tout un peuple*
> *qui ne pouvait plus sortir des faubourgs*
> *Et ces mains semblables à un couvent sans jardin!* . . .
> *Et celles qui m'enfermaient*
> *comme une troupe de malades*
> *dans une serre un jour de pluie!* . . .
> *Oh! j'ai connu d'étranges attouchements!*
> *Et voici qu'ils m'entourent à jamais!*[5]

It is from this same angle, it seems to us, that Mallarmé's final

---

3. André Gide, *Les Cahiers d'André Walter*, p. 149. See also "Lettre," *O.C.*, II, 481-2.

4. Jules Laforgue, *Le Sanglot de la terre, O.C.*, I, 24.

5. Maurice Maeterlinck, *Serres chaudes*, p. 84-5.

attempt to represent the absolute should be viewed. "Un Coup de dés jamais n'abolira le hasard" (1897), a supplement to his *Igitur*, appearing after an interval of thirty years, is not the work of a "mystificateur" but of a "désespéré." In it Mallarmé commemorates the shipwreck of man in his voyage toward the absolute, toward "l'unique nombre qui ne peut être un autre:"[6] a voyage without instrument, without direction, toward a star which is pictured not only beyond physical reach but beyond spiritual comprehension. The throwing of the dice, of which we had the initial example in *Igitur*, is the representation of human power, and the "hasard," which it cannot succeed in mastering, the force that controls the absolute. Here again it is the word "Rien" that dominates Mallarmé's obscure imagery. Placed at the top of a page, isolated from homelier, more human linguistic expressions, immense in its nudity, it displays in its tremendous nihilism the futility of human effort: "Rien n'aura eu lieu que le lieu inférieur clapotin pour disperser l'acte vide abruptement qui sinon par son mensonge eût fondé la perdition."[6]

In the same way, it is the desolation of the word "rien" which in "Le Pasteur des montagnes" expresses Saint-Pol-Roux' realization of the failure of the attempt to be "voyant:" "On n'a rien vu. A peine les ébats d'un puceron sur l'infini de l'Espace et du Temps."[7]

Gide blames the impossibility of attaining freedom not on exterior obstacles, but—what is more despairing—on man's inner incapacity: "L'ennemi est en nous voilà le terrible. La fuite n'est pas possible. On s'inquiète, on erre, on se désespère.[8] And, supplementing this thought in *Les Nourritures terrestres,* he claims that all human liberty is an illusion: "Des livres m'avaient montré chaque liberté provisoire et qu'elle n'est jamais que de choisir son esclavage, ou du moins sa dévotion."[9]

Even Apollinaire, who displayed optimism and confidence in human capacity to conquer the unknown, in "Les Collines," had moments of great despair when he pictured himself as an Icarus, falling empty handed from the forbidden heights. Labeling this fall "L'Ignorance" he said:

6. Stephane Mallarmé, *Un Coup de dés jamais n'abolira le hasard,* pages not numbered.
7. Saint-Pol-Roux, *Les Reposoirs de la procession,* I, 232-3.
8. Gide, *Les Cahiers d'André Walter,* p. 128.
9. Gide, *Les Nourritures terrestres,* p. 114.

Icare

Mais, ton amour, soleil, brûlé divinement
Mon corps qu'être divin voulut mon ignorance

Bateliers

Un dieu choit dans la mer, un dieu nu, les mains vides.[10]

And in another poem, entitled "Sanglot," he sums up this despair as:

Tu ne briseras pas la chaîne de ces causes
Et rien ne sera libre jusqu'à la fin des temps
Laissons tout aux morts
Et cachons nos sanglots[11]

In *Le Poète assassiné* he went as far as to compare the whole poetic effort to "une profonde statue en rien."[12]

With the advent of the catastrophe of war, the counterforce of nihilism, which had risen out of the search for the absolute, dominated more and more those who had not yet found their direction as artists. The "rien," previously heard intermittently, became the rallying point of a nationally and individually varied group. They saw around them war, treating the sensitive and callous alike, preparing the same end or "néant" for the intelligent and the imbecile. Some went as far as to believe that a greater percentage of fatality had resulted among intellectuals on the battlefield than among those of average mentality. Thence, they felt that the post-war world was left to the colorless uniformity of the unintelligent. In the February 1920 number of the magazine "391," this is how George Ribemont-Dessaignes summed it up:

L'heure est aux héros. Et quels héros! Tous ceux qui avaient du courage sont morts, et quelques autres aussi qui n'en avaient pas, et entre la révolte et la mort ont choisi le hasard de celle-ci, comme plus facile. La proportion d'intellectuels tués est plus forte que celle d'intellectuels revenus le corps étant chez eux plus passifs. De sorte que parmi les sains et saufs, il y a une majorité d'imbéciles.[13]

10. Apollinaire, *Il y a*, p. 81.
11. *Ibid.*, p. 109. See also André Salmon, *Créances*, p. 85.
12. Apollinaire, *Le Poète assassiné*, p. 115.
13. Georges-Ribemont-Dessaignes, *391*, no. 11, no page numbers. See also

What had given substance to the development of the mysticism of the poets from 1870 on, had been their willingness to compromise with reason to the extent of making use of a minimum of linguistic logic to express their vision, situated beyond the barriers of logical thinking. But with this increasing disdain of their fellowmen, a coterie of youths, backed by the inspiration and even support of the older generation,[14] were willing and even eager to break off completely any contact with a public other than themselves and their initiates; for they felt the wrong kind of art had spoiled the general receptivity of the people. As one of their leaders, Francis Picabia, expressed it: "Les hommes sont épuisés par l'art;"[15] the public, according to them, had been benumbed by too much art and led astray by the false art of abstraction. In speaking of the artist and his search for a public, Georges Ribemont-Dessaignes said: "on mène le peuple à l'abstraction . . . Ça sent la mort."[16] If, therefore, this young coterie ever invited the public to its manifestations and exhibitionism, it was only to mock its audience. For, what these youths illustrated in the presence of this detested public was the double meaning of their existence: the passion for freedom and the realization of the impossibility to find a concrete representation of the absolute; that was the chief message of Tristan Tzara's 1916 manifesto: "nous savons sagement . . . que nous ne sommes pas libres et crions liberté."[17]

Seated in a café in Zurich, three of these fanatics had chosen a word to represent this double significance: Dada, a word free of restricted connotations, independent of defined objects, yet potent in its primitiveness, even as the first cries of a child whose longing, as expressed by the word, encompasses all and nothing at the same time: a word that was as meaningless, as useless as the desire that compelled these three to look for it! "Dada est un personnage sans

Lettres de guerre by Jacques Vaché—he wrote to André Breton at the time of the armistice: "Comment vai-je [sic] faire, pauvre ami, pour supporter ces derniers mois d'uniforme? . . . Pourvu qu'ils ne me décervèlent pas pendant qu'Ils m'ont en leur pouvoir." p. 25.

14. For details of the history of Dadaism see reviews: *Dada, Sic, Nord-Ouest, 291, 391, Littérature*; for summary of personnel and activities see Georges Lemaître, *From Cubism to Surrealism.*

15. Francis Picabia, *391*, no. 12, mars 1920.

16. Ribemont-Dessaignes, *op. cit.*, pages not numbered.

17. Tristan Tzara, *Sept manifestes*, p. 11.

figure, un visage sans traits et sans yeux. Un heureux moteur de
plaisir pour l'imagination, un délassement salutaire pour l'esprit."[18]
Whereas "Rien" had been a symbol of frustration, now it was to be
glorified, be made not the obstacle but the goal of artistic propens-
sities: "Dada, lui, ne veut rien, rien, rien. . . . Les Dadaists ne sont
rien, rien, rien, bien certainement ils n'arriveront à rien, rien, rien—
signé Francis Picabia qui ne sait rien, rien, rien."[19] Or as Eluard expressed it: "Nous ne faisons Rien, satisfaction Dada."[20] And, whereas
"le hasard" had been challenged as the force that prevented the
artist from organizing his absolute image, the futility of his strife
was now turned into a worship of this chaotic force of the universe.
If the will had proved incompetent to control "le hasard" through
its "coup de dés," it would let the "hasard" master its field of influence. Art would become the seventh side of the die.[21] If art could
not assimilate something of the power of mystical chance, it would
let this same chance engulf its personality; if this unfathomable
"rien" or "absolu" could not submit to representation through the
concrete realities within reach of the artist, then the artist was willing to let these concrete realities vanish into this "rien" and thus
find their moment of absolute existence in the moment of their de-
composition and destruction. It is upon this philosophy that all the
fantastic and outwardly supercilious manifestoes and demonstrations
of the Dadaists were based: the purpose of their "art," collage, is
but to give a free course to the powers of "le hasard," whose unlimited fields of actions are regarded as the very antithesis of the
restricted action of the human mind.

Seizing upon the very characteristics which we have seen forming
the groundwork of the seekers of the absolute, the Dadaists abused
them to such an extent that they were reduced to the chaos from
which they had sprung.

Dehumanization? Yes, indeed! Freedom lay beyond the human element; therefore, divinity was not only to become synonymous with
*de*humanization but was to be identified with "l'anti-humain:" "ce qu'il

18. Marie de la Hire, "Croquis Dada," *391,* no. 14, novembre 1920.

19. Picabia, *391,* no. 12, mars 1920.

20. Paul Eluard, "Cinq moyens pénurie Dada ou deux mots d'explication,"
Littérature, 2ᵉ Année, XIII, 20.

21. "La Septième face du dé" is the title given by George Hugnet to the
Dadaist work upon which he collaborated with Marcel Duchamp.

y a de divin en nous est l'éveil de l'action anti-humaine. . . . Que chaque homme crie: il y a un grand travail destructif, négatif à accomplir. Balayer, nettoyer."[22] For these extremists the act of transforming was the work of weaklings; it was not enough to want to *change* life, one had to be willing not only to break with humanity, but to oppose it, to defile it, to do away with all aspects of it if possible:

> Plus de peintres, plus de littérateurs, plus de musiciens, plus de sculpteurs, plus de religions, plus de républicains, plus de royalistes, plus d'impérialistes, plus d'anarchistes, plus de socialistes, plus de bolchéviques, plus de prolétaire, plus de démocrates, plus de bourgeois, plus d'aristocrates, plus d'armes, plus de police, plus de patries, enfin assez de toutes les imbécilités, plus rien, plus rien, *rien, rien, rien.*[23]

And, to go still farther, why look upon a world that is simply *de*humanized? Rather, replace the human by something that will show man to be ludicrous. In painting, this could be done by reducing the human element to something totally mechanical, inanimate! Such was, for instance, Marcel Duchamp's "Nude descending the stairs." In literature, it meant a detour to Lautréamont's violence and Alfred Jarry's impudence. In the process of destruction all that was to be left of man were his excrements.

Man was an entity whose wellbeing was centered around the gregarious instinct, expressed by his love of his fellowmen. Everything, therefore, that pertained to his love of society was to be denied: family, home, country, and the pursuit of the harmony of happiness,[24] which earlier Lautréamont, and Rimbaud had sought to undermine. Already on the eve of Dadaism, André Gide had given expression to this anti-social attitude in *Les Nourritures terrestres.*[25] He had warned Nathanaël that: "Rien n'est plus dangereux pour toi

22. "Manifeste Dada," *Dada 3,* décembre 1918.

23. "Manifeste du Mouvement Dada," *Littérature,* XIII, 1.

24. In his analysis of the post war generation, Daniel-Rops sees as one of the characteristics of the entire generation this refusal of happiness: "Cette inacceptation du bonheur, du calme, de la paix, il va de soi qu'elle se montre surtout dans les rapports de ces jeunes hommes avec les femmes de leur génération," *Les Années tournantes,* p. 47.

25. Daniel-Rops points out the influence of the *Nourritures terrestres* on the generation of 1918. See p. 43.

que *ta* famille, que *ta* chambre, que *ton* passé."[26] And more vehemently he had repeated: "Familles, je vous hais! foyers clos; portes refermées; possessions jalouses du bonheur."[27]

This was assumed as the credo of all the Dadaists. André Breton gave it its most vivid expression:

> *Lâchez tout*
> *Lâchez Dada*
> *Lâchez votre femme, lâchez votre maîtresse*
> *Lâchez vos espérances et vos craintes*
> *Semez vos enfants au coin d'un bois*
> *Lâchez la proie pour l'ombre*
> *Lâchez au besoin une vie aisée;*
> *ce qu'on vous donne pour une situation d'avenir*
> *Partez sur les routes.*[28]

Man was an entity whose existence was based on balance. Balance, therefore, was to be hated and spurned. Apollinaire's *Le Poète assassiné* appearing on the eve of this dadaist epoch (1916), glorified physical disequilibrium as "divine." His "Infirme divinisé" had lost in an accident one leg, one arm, one eye, one ear. Instead of making him inferior to the rest of humanity, this infirmity had made him superhuman by liberating him from the human notion of time, and making him sense, instead, eternity:

> A vrai dire, il semble impossible de croire qu'elles [his actions] lui parussent simultanées et le seul mot qui, dans la pensée des hommes accoutumés à l'idée du temps, puisse rendre ce qui se passait dans le cerveau de Justin Couchot est celui d'éternité. Ses actions, ses gestes, les impressions qui frappaient son œil, son oreille uniques lui semblaient éternelles et ses membres solitaires étaient impuissants à créer pour lui, entre les divers actes de la vie, cette liaison que deux jambes, deux bras, deux oreilles suscitent dans l'esprit des hommes normaux et de quoi résulte la notion du temps.
>
> Bizarre infirmité, qui méritait qu'on l'appelât divine![29]

---

26. Gide, *Les Nourritures terrestres,* p. 90. The underlining is the author's.
27. *Ibid.,* p. 116.
28. André Breton, *Les Pas perdus,* p. 132.
29. Apollinaire, *Le Poète assassiné,* p. 188-9.

This physical disequilibrium is one of the main characteristics of Dadaist expression: whether in writing, drawing or collages, distorted or dismembered bodies are everywhere evident.

Man was an entity whose greatness had fed upon thought. Mind, therefore, was to be belittled and derided: "Dada travaille avec toutes ses forces à l'instauration de l'idiot partout."[30] Through a distortion of Shakespeare's famous lines:

> *There are more things in heaven and earth, Horatio,*
> *Than are dreamt of in your philosophy*

the Dadaists remarked on the scarcity of meaning in the things of the earth: "Il y a beaucoup moins de choses sur terre que ne nous le fait croire notre philosophie."[31] Since the mind deceived man into thinking that there were more things on earth than there really were, Dada was to have no faith in its data, and was to doubt everything: "Dada doute de tout," said the "Antiphilosophe."[32] "Je détruis les tiroirs du cerveau,"[33] Tzara claimed in his Dada Manifestoes. Since the assumption of the greatness of the human mind was based on its power of logic, to the divinity of physical disequilibrium was to be added that of mental disequilibrium: "La logique est toujours fausse," wrote Tzara.[34] Long association with logic had contaminated, degenerated art, he thought: "Marié à la logique l'art vivait dans l'inceste, engloutissant, avalant sa propre queue toujours son corps."[35] And in 1920 André Breton explained to the readers of *La Nouvelle Revue Française* that all true poets fled the intelligible: "Les poètes . . . fuient sans espoir l'intelligible, ils savent que leur œuvre n'a rien à y perdre. On peut aimer plus qu'aucune autre une femme insensée."[36] Thus, all true Dadaists were to assume the attitude of knowing nothing, thinking nothing. And associating God with what they thought to be the alleged powers of the mind, they would deny Him as well: "Le plus ancien et le plus redoutable ennemi de Dada s'appelle DIEU. . . . Il est le faussaire,

30. T. Tzara, *Sept manifestes Dada*, p. 82.
31. *391*, Numéro 13, juillet 1920, pages not numbered
32. *Bulletin Dada*, no. 6, pages not numbered
33. Tzara, *Sept manifestes Dada*, p. 27.
34. *Ibid.*, p. 32.
35. Tzara, "Manifeste Dada," *Bulletin Dada*, no. 6, pages not numbered.
36. André Breton, "Pour Dada," *NRF*, XV, 1er août, 1920, p. 211.

le spéculateur, le dupeur, le grand forceur, et le suprême truffeur de cervelles."[37]

What was to replace the equilibrium of the mind, then? Thought was now conceived as entirely dominated by sensation and instinct. Already Gide had shown that he found sensation more desirable for man to seek than the abstractions to be found in books:

> . . . *Mais moi j'aime mieux les framboises.*
> *Ça lui a rempli d'amertume les entrailles*
> *Et après il a eu beaucoup de visions.*
> *Nathanaël. Quand aurons-nous brûlé tous les livres! ! !*[38]

The very core of this materialistic mysticism had been the belief that sensation through its more uncontrolled nature was a more adequate conductor toward the grasp of the absolute than abstract, organized thought: "que je boive de quoi redonner à ma chair—et pour libérer mon esprit,—la vision de tout l'ailleurs que je souhaite"[39] was the way Gide might have summarized his *Nourritures terrestres.* We find the same motivation in Apollinaire's "Liens," in which he sees through the exaltation of the senses his only release from the limited reality of ordinary life:

> *J'écris seulement pour vous exalter*
> *O sens, o sens chéris*
> *Ennemis du souvenir*
> *Ennemis du désir*
> *Ennemis du regret*
> *Ennemis des larmes*[40]

Daniel-Rops, in his analysis of the post war generation, deplores this cult of sensation as a definite sign of the disappearance of metaphysical preoccupation in the "années tournantes:"

> Dans ce qu'elle avait de meilleur, cette inquiétude apparaissait comme une interrogation sur le sens de la vie. Or ce sens de la vie étant, chez un très grand nombre, envisagé comme par définition limité à la vie elle-même, je veux dire n'ayant pas à être

37. Paul Dermée, "Dada tue-Dieu," *Littérature,* 2ᵉ Année, XIIII, 13.
38. Gide, *Les Nourritures terrestres, O.C.,* II, p. 76.
39. *Ibid.*
40. Apollinaire, "Liens," *Calligrammes,* p. 14.

justifié sur un plan métaphysique, il était naturel qu'on cher-
chât à le trouver dans le domaine de la plus pure sensation.[41]

That, among the Dadaists, this exaltation of the senses was to be
carried to extremes (which might be considered injecting dangerous
influences in society itself) is quite obvious. But in the light of its
long evolution, it ceases, it seems to me, to appear as a sudden revolt or reaction to the war, and as a loss or absence of mysticism.
On the contrary, it looms out of genuine disgust of tenable, evident
realities, as a peculiar distortion of an intense longing for the unattainable aspects of reality. When Tristan Tzara says in his Manifesto:
"Un tableau est l'art de faire rencontrer deux lignes géométrique-
ment constatées parallèles, sur une toile, devant nos yeux, dans une
réalité qui transpose sur un monde à d'autres conditions et possibilités"[42] it is true that his ideal of art does seem to be based on pure
sensation. But for what purpose? To try to seize through inconceivable sensations "un monde à d'autres conditions et possibilités." And
when he seeks "les champions oranges et la famille des sons du tri-
bord,"[43] he cannot be said to limit his interests to life itself; on the
contrary he shows complete lack of interest in "la vie elle-même" as
Daniel-Rops used the expression.

Marriage of the abstract and the concrete: this procedure, which we
found in symbolism to be based on an inner artistic control and order, and later to be taken by the seekers of the absolute as the basis
for the representation of the absurd, was to be cultivated to a point
where it became not the *means* but the *purpose* of expression:

> J'écris ce manifeste pour montrer qu'on peut faire les actions
> opposées ensemble, dans une seule fraîche respiration; je suis
> contre l'action; pour la continuelle contradiction, pour l'affir-
> mation aussi, je ne suis ni pour ni contre et je n'explique pas car je
> hais le bon-sens. . . . Ordre=désordre, moi=non-moi, affir-
> mation=négation; *rayonnements suprêmes d'un art absolu.*[44]

No longer can the reader distinguish the poles of the contradiction

41. Daniel Rops, *Les Années tournantes,* p. 41.
42. Tzara, "Manifeste Dada," *Dada 3,* décembre 1918, pages not numbered.
43. Tzara, *La Première Aventure céleste de M. Antipyrine, Petite Anthologie
poétique du surréalisme,* p. 127.
44. Tzara, "Manifeste Dada," *Dada 3,* décembre 1918, pp. not numbered.

in this complete, illogical integration of the concrete and the abstract:

> *c'est le troupeau des montagnes en chemise dans notre église qui*
> *est la gare de l'ouest les chevaux se sont pendus à Bucarest en*
> *regardant Mbogo qui monte sur ses bicyclettes tandis que les*
> *cheveux télégraphiques s'enivrent des oreilles du ventriloque*
> *débordent quatre ramoneurs qui*
> *crèvent ensuite comme des melons*
> *le prêtre photographe a accouché de trois enfants striés pareils*
> *aux violons sur la colline poussent des pantalons un histrion de*
> *feuilles lunaires se balance dans son armoire. . . .*
> *nous sommes devenus des reverbères [etc.: six times]*[45]

This is what Apollinaire had predicted when a short while before he had characterized the new poetry as follows: "C'était une poésie pleine de profondeur où tous les mots avaient un sens nouveau. C'est ainsi qu'*archipel* n'était employé par elle que dans le sens de *papier buvard*.[46] This is what Jacques Vaché had envisaged when in 1918 he had written to André Breton: that the purpose of "l'esprit nouveau" should be: "Former la sensation personnelle à l'aide d'une collision flamboyante de mots rares."[47] In short, this complete substitution of contradiction for the old technique of comparison formed the basis of all Dada Manifestoes and other writings; and it was the inevitable result of an utter abandonment of logic:

> La comparaison est un moyen littéraire qui ne nous contente plus. Il ya des moyens de formuler une image ou de l'intégrer, mais les éléments seront pris dans des sphères différentes et éloignées.
>
> La logique ne nous guide plus, et son commerce, bien commode, trop impuissant, lueur trompeuse, semant les monnaies du relativisme, stérilité, est pour nous à jamais éteint.[48]

The incomprehension of the reader in the face of any writing based on this principle would not be considered by the Dadaists as fail-

45. Tzara, *op. cit.*, p. 125.
46. Apollinaire, *Le Poète assassiné*, p. 83.
47. Vaché, *Lettres de guerre*, p. 18.
48. "Note 14 sur la poésie," *Dada 4-5*, not numbered.

ure for themselves but as a definite sign of success. For it is thus
that Tristan Tzara characterized his own work: "Tous mes poèmes
sont des poèmes en forme d'errata."[49] The absurd as manifested by the
use of the wrong word, had thus become the ideal of Dada "poetry,"
and it persisted even after 1920 when with the advent of Surrealism
Dada folded up. In 1928 this "errata" is still very much evident:

> *Il était une grande maison*
> *sur laquelle nageait un scaphandrier de feu . . .*
> *Il était une grande maison*
> *dont le maître était de paille*
> *dont le maître était un hêtre*
> *dont le maître était une lettre*
> *dont le maître était un poil*
> *dont le maître était un soupir*
> *dont le maître était un virage*
> *dont le maître était un vampire*
> *dont le maître était une vache enragée*
> *dont le maître était un coup de pied*
> *dont le maître était une voix caverneuse*
> *dont le maître était une tornade*
> *dont le maître était une barque chavirée*
> *dont le maître était une fesse*
> *dont le maître était la Carmagnole*
> *dont le maître était la mort violente*
> *Dites-moi dites-moi où est la grande maison*[50]

What of the *cult of the future* and the desire to assume the role of
prophets? Like the seekers of the absolute, the Dadaists disclaimed
memory. Not only did they renounce the faculty of remembering
but showed hostility toward the entire concept of honoring the past
accomplishments of humanity. It is the art of forgetting that they
would have liked to cultivate. But this disdain of memory was not to
turn the Dadaists toward an energetic contemplation of the future.
The end of the war had not brought about the justification of the
optimism that had counteracted despair during the war. The Dada-

49. Tzara, "M.Aa l'Antiphilosophe," *391*, no. 13.
50. Benjamin Péret, *Le Grand Jeu, Petite Anthologie poetique du surréalisme*,
p. 114.

ists could not believe in social progress: "il serait ridicule d'attendre un chef-d'œuvre Dada. Nous ne croyons non plus naturellement, à la possibilité d'aucune amélioration sociale."[51] Nor did they believe in artistic immortality; Breton characterized the expectations of Dada as follows: "Dada ne se donne à rien, ni à l'amour, ni au travail. Il est inadmissible qu'un homme laisse une trace de son passage sur la terre."[52] Along with all the abolitions they preached, the Dadaists advocated the "abolition du futur:"

> Tout produit du dégoût susceptible de devenir une négation de la famille, est *dada*; proteste aux poings de tout son être en action destructive: *dada* . . . dada; abolition de la logique . . . *Dada*; abolition de la mémoire: Dada; abolition des prophètes: Dada, abolition du futur . . . Liberté: Dada, dada, dada, hurlement des couleurs crispées, entrelacement des contraires et de toutes les contradictions, des grotesques, des inconséquences. La Vie.[53]

Thus, the future was also to enter within the orbit of "rien!" For many, then, the Road to the Absolute was to lead into complete renunciation, to complete chaos: chaos of art, chaos of thought, chaos of life itself.

But this collective pessimism was a far cry from the picture that Gonzague Truc was painting of the "jeunes gens d'aujourd'hui" in his *Crise intellectuelle*, written in 1919:

> Le matérialisme scientiste apportait sa commode et superficielle réponse aux questions que la vie se pose sur la vie; on se contentait de ses décisions, et, puisqu'il nous réduisait à la terre, on se consolait assez volontiers de ne vivre que pour ici-bas.
>
> Ainsi se formait une sorte de barbarie confortable et relativement policée qui continue de se façonner sous nos yeux. Nul souci métaphysique ou religieux ne hante plus les âmes, si l'on peut dire qu'il y ait encore des âmes.[54]

On the contrary, as far as the artistic nature of the young blood was concerned, the decisions of materialism had been far from content-

---

51. Breton, "Patinage Dada," *Littérature*, 2ᵉ Année, XIII, 9.
52. *Ibid.*, p. 18.
53. Tzara, "Manifeste Dada," *Dada 3*, décembre 1918.
54. Gonzague Truc, *Une Crise intellectuelle*, pp. 28-9.

ing it and compelling it to accept the "ici-bas." Rather, their "souci métaphysique" had become so acute that from it had resulted not only complete disgust with ordinary life, but also the conviction that art had proved inadequate in transforming nature and human experience. As Jacques Rivière pointed out in his article "Reconnaissance à Dada"—and as I have tried to show in detail in this study: "Tout ce que disent et prétendent les Dada il y a longtemps que toute une lignée d'écrivains s'appuie dessus."[55] If Rivière felt gratitude toward Dada it was because he saw in these expressions and manifestations the first conscious realization of essential dogmas that the entire literature of the last hundred years had implied and indicated.[56]

If the Dadaists sought to place themselves beyond the control of Beauty and its rules, it was because of their inner consciousness of something greater. Guillaume Apollinaire created in his description of himself and André Salmon, the perfect characterization of the Dadaists: "pèlerins de la perdition:"[57] "pilgrims" because of the dangerous path on which they ventured with almost religious fervor, "perdition" because it was into chaos that these dreams led them. To them art was not a means to personal glory and power; for it they were willing to risk all because in all that was around them they saw nothing of value. To them the most hateful spectacle of all was that of a successful artist. Their own artistic experiment demanded almost as complete loss of personal identity as in the field of scientific research. Many of the Dada writings were anonymous, and there was such a unity of purpose, unity of thought, unity of nihilism among the members of the group that it would have been possible to attribute any one writing to any one individual in the clan. As they claimed in *391*, one of their many short-lived magazines, they were truly all Presidents of the Dada coterie. They contributed equally to the eloquent failure of their work, as, from the Tower of Babel they had built, they fell—inarticulate!

55. Jacques Rivière, "Reconnaissance à Dada," *Nouvelle Revue Française* ler août, 1920, p. 223.
56. See *supra*, Introduction, p. 4.
57. Apollinaire, "Poème lu au mariage d'André Salmon," *Alcools*, p. 67.

Envoi

*Mais en Europe on défait la nuit la toile que le jour a tissée;
on éprouve d'autres fils, on ourdit d'autres trames, et chaque
matin résonne le bruit des métiers qui fabriquent du nouveau,
en trépidant.*

—Paul Hazard

DID the iconoclasts of the last seventy-five years seriously shake the traditional values of French poetry: order, moderation, regularity of form, linguistic impeccability, and social consciousness?

Let us not forget that Paul Valéry's limpid logic and precise perfection can also proceed from Mallarmé, and Paul Claudel's overwhelming religious exaltation from Rimbaud. Extremists, faltering between the absolute and chaos, by no means monopolized the resources of poetic mysticism. From Romanticism, which Baudelaire characterized as being essentially an "aspiration vers l'infini,"[1] another route could be traced leading to a different type of "spiritual conquest"[2] of the universe: a search for the absolute which implied neither revolt against nature nor disdain of humanity.

Certainly Europe does not bend all its energies to the execution of a single canvas. But in creating multitudinous tapestries, it sometimes builds a new pattern by reverting to the substance of an older one. The Romantic tradition is aglow with new color in the hands of Paul Claudel. The alliance of heaven and earth has not been abandoned as a futile dream. Claudel has taken up the mystic visions of Lamartine, Balzac, Hugo; he has intensified them with his passionate desire to include the whole world of matter within the aureole of the absolute. But he has not deviated from the stabilizing forces that guarded the Romanticists, on their hazardous journey, from the precipices of Dada.

1. C. Baudelaire, *Variétés critiques*, I, 9.
2. P. Claudel, Préface, *Œuvres complètes*, Rimbaud.

It is with the poetry of Claudel that the essential characteristics of French Romantic mysticism culminate: the refusal to subordinate the divine to the human, repudiation of chance, and glorification of human values. While the Surrealists flung protest upon protest against the forces that made of man the slave of gravitation, Claudel joyfully accepts, as the will of God, the uncontrollable powers of the universe—whether they bring good or evil to humanity. The Job-like faith which made Lamartine write:

> *Mais c'est Dieu qui t'écrase, ô mon âme, sois forte!*
> *Baise sa main sous la douleur*[3]

rises to an even more powerful resignation in the blissful prayer that the bereaved Anne Vercors of *L'Annonce faite à Marie* offers to God before His "table desservie."[4] The Surrealists found the laws of chance in contradiction to those of human reason and pictured art either as a struggle against objective hazard or a yielding on the part of the human will to the illogical caprices of chance; Claudel, like Balzac, who believed in a superior causality and in the power of the artist's will over chance,[5] envisages a logical and continuous pattern in the universe:

> Et ne parlez pas de hasard. La plantation de ce bouquet de pins, la forme de cette montagne n'en sont pas plus l'effet que le Parthenon ou ce diamant sur qui vieillit le lapidaire à l'user, mais le produit d'un trésor de desseins certes plus riche et plus savant.[6]

The Surrealists found evil, idiocy and disorder in the recesses of human sensibility; in exploring the hidden forces of nature, Claudel, too, came upon the sources of evil, but like Hugo—and with more conviction—he envisaged the ultimate triumph of good, by attributing to humanity the will to maintain equilibrium and an infinite capacity for love:

---

3. See for development of this theme in Lamartine's poetry: Henri Guillemin, *Le Jocelyn de Lamartine,* "Message et Secrets de Jocelyn."
4. P. Claudel, *L'Annonce faite à Marie,* p. 207.
5. For analysis of this phase of Balzac's work see: F. Baldensperger, *Orientations étrangères,* "La Répudiation du hasard."
6. Claudel, *Art poétique:* "Connaissance du temps," pp. 51-2.

. . . Notre occupation pour l'éternité sera l'accomplissement de notre part dans la perpétuation de l'Office, le maintien de notre équilibre toujours nouveau dans un immense tact amoureux de tous nos frères, l'élévation de notre voix, dans l'inénarrable gémissement de l'Amour.[7]

Here, then, is a mysticism that is revealed in a representation of life, diagonally opposed to that of the Surrealists. The world is as new as on the day of its creation:

Ouvrez les yeux! Le monde est encore intact; il est vierge comme au premier jour, frais comme le lait! L'inconnu est la matière de notre connaissance, il est le bien de notre esprit et sa chère nourriture. Les hommes antérieurs n'ont point endommagé notre droit, ils n'ont point réduit notre patrimoine.[8]

Nothing is too high nor too profound for mankind:

Inconnu des hommes, l'Etre qui nous a créés et nous
conserve en nous considérant
Nous connaît, et nous contribuons secrètement à sa gloire.[9]

The essence of existence and creation is movement: ". . . Le mouvement est . . . l'impossibilité pour le mobile de *subsister,* de garder la place qu'il occupait; il tend de *nature* à s'en éloigner, il fait effort pour fuir. . . . Tout mouvement a pour résultat la création ou le maintien d'un état d'équilibre." [10]

Both these aspects of poetic mysticism are part of the heritage of the twentieth century and are expressions of that "crise de l'esprit"[11] which Paul Valéry symbolized in a Hamlet wavering between order and disorder.

An inevitable question arises: in the light of the sublimity of a Claudel, does the subversiveness of the Surrealists and their precursors seem to be a total loss and even a detriment to art? When time with its ruthless objectivity sweeps away much of the sound and fury, much of the wasted paper and spilled ink, very little may re-

---

7. *Ibid.,* p. 192-3.
8. *Ibid.,* p. 26.
9. Claudel, *La Ville.*
10. Claudel, *op. cit.,* p. 72, p. 75.
11. Paul Valéry, *Variété,* p. 20.

main to which future generations will deign give the name of "art."
The Surrealist "cenacle" has already ceased to exist. There has been
dissension; there have been harsh, ugly words. Much of the eccen-
tricity has been attenuated.[12] A new world catastrophe made some of the
young anarchists of 1920 bards of the Resistance or sober exiles, now
committed to patriotism and belief in divine Providence. There is nothing anti-human, anti-social or anti-emotional in the lyrical anguish with
which Louis Aragon or Paul Eluard voice the mourning or the faith of a
politically defeated France. And in talking with the older Breton of today, one is impressed with the clarity of his discourse, the scope of his
knowledge, the steadiness of his gait. He appears anchored in bourgeois
society; he seems to be seeking roots, orienting himself toward stability;
he wants to be part of a recognized literary tradition; he speaks of his
poetic works as if they had been scientific experiments, and, when questioned on some of the more revolutionary aspects of Surrealism, his eyes
turn to the pictorial representations rather than the literary ones. In fact,
were it not for those paintings which I saw covering the walls of his
home in exile, in New York during World War II, one might be
tempted to say: "Breton has compromised with reality." Upon leaving
him, I had the impression of having questioned a medium after the
tables had ceased turning. . . .

Of the poetic lineage of Surrealism this much at least may be remembered in the years to come: if the human desire to escape physical limitations is an old poetic theme, it nonetheless has undergone
a complete renewal in the last hundred years; it has at times been
crystallized in a mysticism that tends to endow art with an existence
independent of nature and human life:

> C'est cette création qui marquera notre époque. Nous sommes
> à une époque de création artistique . . . où l'on crée des œuvres
> qui, en se détachant de la vie, y rentrent parce qu'elles ont une
> existence propre, en dehors de l'évocation ou de la reproduc-
> tion des choses de la vie.[13]

12. Younger writers—this time dramatists and novelists—are rallying under
the new banner of Existentialism to voice their reaction to another social upheaval
and to shock anew a public which they find ready for a new literary canvas. Another *ism* is born, but it remains to be seen whether it will fuse, as in the case of
Surrealism, into the broader literary trends of French literature or remain a short-
lived, isolated fad.

13. *Nord-Sud* "Sur le cubisme," no. 3, 15 mai 1917, p. 11.

If, by attacking reason, the poet tried to shake the very foundations of literature, and if he defied the dignity of human thought, he paradoxically attributed to the mind an inconceivable power: that of freeing itself from nature.

Needless to say the venture could not succeed. But this much will remain: this strange, atheistic mysticism introduced into French poetry the "appétit de néant"[14] for which French poetry had so long been considered inept by many of its critics. Three generations of poets succeeded gradually in giving an intense reality to this "néant" by associating it with concrete entities rather than relegating it to formless abstractions. They prevented poetic mysticism from becoming confused with philosophical speculation, as it might have been, had it followed too closely the epic genre of Hugo. The object was given a fourth dimension rather than man a sixth sense. Poets gradually developed an idiom which might be used to express the human concept of the absolute; they tried to realize Baudelaire's dream: "de la langue et de l'écriture, prises comme opérations magiques, sorcellerie évocatoire."[15] Although much of this poetic language is ugly, discordant, distasteful, it has an amazing scope of imagery, which at moments seems to reveal a world indeed deprived of the elements of time, space and movement. By accepting the contradictory and the absurd, the poet appears to have succeeded in freeing the metaphor from its conventional structure, and poetry from the "cheville." The originality of a Paul Eluard derives from the workshops of a long line of rebels:

> Denise disait aux merveilles:
>
> *Le soir, un rien, une hirondelle qui dépasse,*
> *Un peu de vent, les feuilles qui ne tombent plus,*
> *Un beau détail, un sortilège sans vertus*
> *Pour un regard qui n'a jamais compris l'espace.*[16]

> Mascha riait aux anges:
>
> *L'heure qui tremble au front du temps tout embrouillé*
> *Un bel oiseau léger plus vif qu'une poussière*
> *Traîne sur un miroir un cadavre sans tête*
> *Des boules de soleil adoucissent ses ailes*
> *Et le vent de son vol affole la lumière* [17]

14. See P. Hazard, *Quatre études*, p. 57.
15. C. Baudelaire, *Fusées*, p. 82.
16. P. Eluard, *Mourir de ne pas mourir*, p. 35.
17. *Ibid.*, p. 50.

Those who revolted against both the greatness and the insignificance of human effort, have left in their stammering and brutal documents a vivid image of the complexity of modern man and of the contradictions that constitute society today; degeneration coupled with a constant power of renewal and change; satiety and an unrelenting cult of sensation; intense desire to come to greater grips with the organic world and a mystical longing to transform the inanimate; a terrifying passion spent upon annihilating all human emotion; a powerful lucidity serving to bring to light the illogical forces of the subconscious. From these works emerges the portrait of an extreme individualist who loses his "I" in the very forces of the "néant" he has explored. Out of these protests rises the figure of an artist who seeks a more potent Word, while showing skeptical disconcern over its immortality.

Is there in all the documents grouped in this study a conscious and continuous pattern? Or have I tried to fashion a synthetic structure out of miscellany? At moments one becomes skeptical about classification and synthesis in dealing with the poetic genre. It is as if we had tried to hold water in our hands; all that remains is the trace of its passage—the dampness, the unsatisfying moisture. . . .

A poem of W. H. Auden comes to mind:

> *For poetry makes nothing happen it survives*
> *In the valley of its saying where executives*
> *Would never want to tamper; it flows south*
> *From ranches of isolation and the busy griefs,*
> *Raw towns that we believe and die in; it survives*
> *A way of happening, a mouth.*[18]

The presence of these fragments of poetic thought create the moving spectacle one might witness if on the shores of the Aegean sea one were to come upon the broken wings of Icarus. And who can say whether from the debacle of the present may not rise the sky-reaching instrument of the future!

18. W. H. Auden, *Memory of W. B. Yeats.*

Bibliography

I: SOURCE MATERIAL

Anthologie de la nouvelle poésie française, Paris, KRA, 1928.

Apollinaire, Guillaume, *Alcools,* Paris, Mercure de France, 1913, (Nouvelle Revue Française, 1927).

————*Calligrammes,* Paris, Mercure de France, 1918, (Nouvelle Revue Française, 1936).

————*L'Enchanteur pourrissant,* Paris, Henry Kahnweiler, 1909, (Nouvelle Revue Française, 1921).

————*Il y a,* Paris, Messein, 1925.

————*Les Mamelles de Tirésias,* drame surréaliste, Paris, Editions Sic, 1918.

————*Le Poète assassiné,* Paris, L'Edition, 1914, (Au Sans Pareil, 1927).

Aragon, Louis, *Painting and Reality,* (James J. Sweeney, translator, Jan. 1937), from "Maison de Culture," May 1936.

————*Le Paysan de Paris,* Paris, Nouvelle Revue Française, 1926.

————*La Peinture au défi,* Paris, Goemans, 1930.

————*Traité du style,* Paris, Nouvelle Revue Française, 1928.

Arnim, Ludwig Achim von, *Sämtliche Werke,* Berlin, Arnim, 1857. "Isabella von Aegypten," I, "Die Majorats-Herren," II.

————*Contes bizarres,* Théophile Gautier, fils, translator, 1856, (Ed. des Cahiers Libres, Paris, 1933).

Baudelaire, Charles, *Les Fleurs du mal,* Paris, Poulet-Mallasis, 1857, (Garnier).

————*Nouvelles Histoires extraordinaires,* par Edgar Poe, Paris, Michel Lévy, 1858, (*Œuvres complètes,* X, Nouvelle Revue Française, 1928).

————*Œuvres posthumes et correspondance inédite,* Paris, Quantin, 1887.

——*Les Paradis artificiels, Le Spleen de Paris,* Paris, Poulet-Mallasis, 1860, (Librairie Gründ).

——"Projet de dédicace pour la seconde édition," *Œuvres complètes,* II, Nouvelle Revue Française, 1933-4).

——"Puisque réalisme il y a," *Mesure,* 4e Année, no. 3, (15 juillet, 1938).

——*Salon de 1845,* Paris, Labitte, 1845.

——*Variétés critiques,* Paris, Michel-Lévy, 1868, (G. Crès, 1924).

Breton, André, 1. *Les Champs magnétiques* (in collaboration with P. Soupault), Paris, Au Sans Pareil, 1920.

——2. *Clair de Terre,* Paris, Collection Littérature, 1923.

——3. *Introduction au discours sur le peu de réalité,* Paris, (Nouvelle Revue Française, 1927.)

——4. *L'Immaculée conception* (in collaboration with P. Eluard), Paris, Editions Surréalistes, 1930.

——5. *Légitime défense,* Paris, Editions Surréalistes, 1926.

——6. *Manifeste du surréalisme, Poisson soluble,* Paris, KRA, 1924.

——7. *Misère de la poésie,* Paris, Editions Surréalistes, 1932.

——8. *Mont-de-Piété,* Paris, Au Sans Pareil, 1919.

——9. *Nadja,* Paris, Nouvelle Revue Française, 1928.

——10. *Les Pas Perdus,* Paris, Nouvelle Revue Française, 1924.

——11. *Notes sur la poésie* (in collaboration with P. Eluard), Paris, Editions G.L.M., 1936.

——12. *Qu'est-ce que le surréalisme,* Brussels, René Henriquez, 1934.

——13. *Second manifeste du surréalisme,* Paris, KRA, 1930.

——14. *Le Surréalisme et la Peinture,* Paris, Nouvelle Revue Française, 1928.

——15. *Les Vases communicants,* Paris, Ed. Cahiers Libres, 1932.

——16. *What is Surrealism?* (including article: "Beauty will be convulsive") David Gascogne, translator, London, Faber, 1936.

Char, René, *Ralentir travaux,* (in collaboration with A. Breton, & P. Eluard), Paris, Editions Surréalistes, 1930.

Crevel, René, *Le Clavecin de Diderot,* Paris, Editions Surréalistes, 1932.

——*L'Esprit contre la raison,* Marseille, Cahiers du Sud, 1927.

——*Etes-vous fou?* Paris, Nouvelle Revue Française, 1929.

——*Mon Corps et moi,* Paris, KRA, 1925.

——*La Mort difficile,* Paris, KRA, 1926.

Cros, Charles, "Les Poèmes, ce sont des plaintes," *Mercure de France,* CXXXI.

De Quincey, Thomas, *Confessions of an Opium Eater,* London Magazine, 1821, (*Collected Writings,* III, Edinburgh, A. & C. Black, 1889-90).

Ducasse, Isidore (Comte de Lautréamont) *Les Chants de Maldoror,* Paris, A. Lacroix, 1869 (not sold until 1879) (*Œuvres complètes,* Paris, Agence Centrale de Librairie, 1938).

———*Préface aux Poésies,* Paris, Librairie Gabrie, 1870. (*O.C.* see above).

Eluard, Paul, *Les Animaux et leurs hommes,* Paris, Au Sans Pareil, 1920.

———*Capitale de la douleur,* Paris, Nouvelle Revue Française, 1926.

———*Défense de savoir,* Paris, Editions Surréalistes, 1928.

———*Les Dessous d'une vie ou La Pyramide humaine,* Marseille, Cahiers du Sud, 1926.

———*Dors,* Paris, privately printed, 1931.

———*L'Immaculée Conception,* see Breton, 4.

———*Les Malheurs des immortels* (in collaboration with Max Ernst) Paris, Librairie Six, 1922.

———*Mourir de ne pas mourir,* Paris, Nouvelle Revue Française, 1924.

———*Les Nécessités de la vie et les Conséquences des rêves,* Paris, Au Sans Pareil, 1921.

———*Notes sur la poésie,* see Breton, 11.

———*Ralentir Travaux,* see Char.

Gautier, Théophile, "Le Club des haschischins," *Revue des Deux Mondes,* 1er février, 1846 (*Œuvres: Romans et Contes,* Paris, Lemerre, 1897).

Ghil, René, "Les Villages des eaux," *Vers et Prose,* XXVIII.

Gide, André, *Les Cahiers d'André Walter. Poèmes,* Paris, Perrin, 1891, (*Œuvres complètes,* Nouvelle Revue Française, I).

———*Les Nourritures terrestres,* Paris, Mercure de France, 1897, (*O.C.,* see above, II).

———*Le Voyage d'Urien,* Paris, Librairie de l'Art Indépendant, 1893, (*O.C.,* see above, I).

Goncourt, E. & J., *Journal,* III, Paris, Flammarion, 1891 (1935).

Hardenberg (Novalis) *Hymnen an die Nacht,* Athenaeum, III, 1800, (*Novalis Schriften,* I, Leipzig, Bibliographisches Institut, 1929).

Hölderlin, Friedrich, *Gedichte und Briefe,* Paul Franke, 1923.

——*Gesammelte Dichtungen,* I, Stuttgart, Cotten, 1898.

Hugnet, George, *La Septième Face du dé,* Paris, Jeanne Bucher, 1936.

Hugo, Victor, *Ce que dit la bouche d'ombre, Contemplations,* II, Paris, Michel-Lévy, 1856, (Paris, Ollendorff, 1895).

——*Dieu, Œuvres inédites,* Paris, Hetzel, 1891.

——*Les Quatre Vents de l'esprit,* Paris, A. Lemerre, 1888, (Poésie XVI, Paris, Hetzel, no date).

——*Toute la lyre,* I, *Œuvres inédites,* Paris, Hetzel, 1888, (Paris, Albin-Michel, 1935).

Jarry, Alfred, *Les Minutes de sable mémorial,* Paris, Mercure de France, 1894, (Paris, Fasquelle Editeurs, 1932).

Kahn, Gustave, *Chansons d'amant,* Bruxelles, Lacomblez, 1891, (*Premiers poèmes,* Paris, Mercure de France, 1897).

——*Les Palais nomades,* Paris, Tresse et Stock, 1887, (see above).

Laforgue, Jules, *Les Complaintes,* Paris, Vanier, 1885, (*Œuvres complètes,* 5 vols., Mercure de France, 1922).

——*Le Concile féerique,* Paris, Edition de la Vogue, 1886, (see above).

——*L'Imitation de Notre-Dame,* Paris, Vanier, 1886 (see above).

——*Moralités légendaires,* Paris, Librairie de la Revue Indépendante, 1887, (see above).

Maeterlinck, Maurice, *Serres chaudes,* Paris, Vanier, 1889, (Bruxelles Lacomblez, 1895).

Mallarmé, Stephane, *Authobiographie et bibliographie des poètes maudits,* Paris, Messein, 1924.

——*Un Coup de dés jamais n'abolira le hasard, Cosmopolis,* mai 1897, (Nouvelle Revue Française, 1914).

——*Igitur,* Paris, Nouvelle Revue Française, 1925.

——*Les Poésies de Stéphane Mallarmé,* Paris, Revue Indépendante, 1887.

Mesens, E., *Alphabet sourd aveugle,* Bruxelles, Editions Nicolas Flamel, 1933.

Monnier, Antoine, *Le Haschisch,* Paris, Willem, 1877.

Nerval, Gérard de, *Aurélia,* (*Le Rêve et la vie, etc.*) Paris, Victor Lecou, 1855, (Paris, Le Divan, 1928).

——*Les Filles du feu,* Paris, D. Giraud, 1854, (Le Divan, 1927).

——*Voyage en Orient,* Paris, H. Souverain, 1850, (Le Divan, 2 vols., 1927).

Petite Anthologie poétique du surréalisme, (ed. George Hugnet), Paris, Jeanne Bucher, 1934.

Picabia, Francis, "Pensées et souvenirs," *Littérature,* Nouvelle Série, IV, 13.

————*391,* no. 12, mars 1920.

Régnier, Henri de, *Poèmes,* Paris, Mercure de France, 1907.

Reverdy, Pierre, *Les Epaves du ciel,* Paris, Nouvelle Revue Française, 1924.

Rimbaud, Arthur, *Les Illuminations,* Paris, La Vogue, 1886, (Mercure de France, 1936).

————*Œuvres complètes,* Maesticht, Halcyon press, Stols, 1931.

————*Une Saison en enfer,* Bruxelles, Alliance typographique, Poot & Cie., 1873 (Mercure de France, 1937).

Rolland, Eugène, *Rimes et jeux de l'enfance, Les Littératures populaires de toutes les nations,* XIV, Paris, Maison Neuve, 1881-1903.

Saint-Pol-Roux, *Les Reposoirs de la procession,* Mercure de France, I, 1901, II, 1904, III, 1907.

Sainte-Beuve, Ch. *Contemplations, Poésies complètes,* I, Paris, Lemerre, 1879.

Salmon, André, *Créances,* (including *Dernières Féeries*), Paris, Nouvelle Revue Française, 1926.

Sand, George, *Lettres d'un voyageur,* Paris, Librairie Bonnaire, 1837, (Paris, Lévy, 1869).

Soupault, Philippe, *Les Champs magnétiques,* (see Breton, 1).

————*Lautréamont,* Paris, Ed. Cahiers Libres, 1927.

Supervielle, Jules, *Gravitations,* Paris, Nouvelle Revue Française, 1925, (1932).

————"Voyage en soi, *Poèmes,* Paris, Eugène Figuière, 1919.

Tzara, Tristan, *L'Antitête,* Paris, Editions des Cahiers Libres, 1933.

————*L'Arbre des voyageurs,* Paris, Editions de la Montagne, 1930.

————*De nos oiseaux,* Paris, KRA, 1930.

————*Grains et Issues,* Paris, Denöel et Steele, 1935.

————*L'Homme approximatif,* Paris, Fourcade, 1930.

————*La Première Aventure céleste de M. Antipyrine,* Zurich, Collection Dada, 1916.

————*Sept Manifestes Dada,* Paris, Jean Budry, 1924.

————*Vingt-cinq Poèmes,* Zurich, Dada, 1918.

Vaché, Jacques, *Lettres de guerre,* Paris, Au Sans Pareil, 1919.

Villiers de l'Isle-Adam, *Axël*, 1890, (*Œuvres complètes*, IV, Paris, Mercure de France, 1923).

Miscellaneous material pertaining to Dadaism and Surrealism: *Nord-Sud* (1917), *Sic.* (1917-18), *Dada* (1917-19), *Littérature* (1917), *Révolution Surréaliste*, (1924-29), *Le Surréalisme au Service de la Révolution* (1933-34).

II: CRITICAL WORKS CONSULTED

Apollinaire, Guillaume, "L'Esprit nouveau et les poètes," *Mercure de France*, 1er décembre, 1918.

Aragon, Louis to Albert Thibaudet (open letter), *Nouvelle Revue Française*, 1er avril, 1922.

Baldensperger, Fernand, *Orientations étrangères chez Honoré de Balzac*, Paris, Champion, 1927.

Barre, André, *Le Symbolisme*, Paris, Jouve & Cie, 1911.

Baruzi, Joseph, *La Volonté de métamorphose*, Paris, Grasset, 1911.

Béguin, Albert, *L'Ame romantique et le Rêve*, 2 vols., Nogent-le-Rotrou, (France) Daupeley-Gouverneur, 1937.

Bergson, Henri, "L'Ame et le Corps," *Le Matérialisme actuel*, Paris, Flammarion, 1913.

Berret, Paul, *La Philosophie de Victor Hugo* (1854-1859), Paris, Paulin, 1910.

Berrichon, Paterne, *J. A. Rimbaud, le poète*, Paris, MF, 1912.

Bertaux, Pierre, *Hölderlin, essai de biographie intérieure*, Paris, Hachette, 1936.

Bouvier, Emile, *Initiation à la littérature d'aujourd'hui*, Paris, La Renaissance du Livre, 1929.

Breton, André, (Interview) *View*, October-November 1941.

Breton, André, "Limites, non frontières du surréalisme," *Nouvelle Revue Française*, 1er février, 1937.

Breton, André, "Pour Dada," *Nouvelle Revue Française*, 1er août 1920.

Brunetière, Ferdinand, "Pour le centenaire d'A. Comte" (pamphlet) IX, 1902.

Carré, J. M., *Les Deux Rimbaud*, Paris, Cahiers Libres, 1928.

Carré, J. M., *Lettres de la vie littéraire d'Arthur Rimbaud*," Paris, NRF, 1931.

Cas Lautréamont, Paris-Bruxelles, Le Disque Vert, 1925.

Charcot, J. M., *Leçons sur les maladies du système nerveux*, III, Paris, 1890.

Charcot, J. M., *Iconographie photographique de la Salpêtrière*, (executed by R. Bourneville) 3 vols., Aux Bureaux du Progrès Médical, 1876—1880.

Charpentier, John, *Le Symbolisme*, Paris, Les Arts et le Livre, 1927.

Claudel, Paul, *Positions et propositions* (Préface aux Œuvres d'Arthur Rimbaud) Paris, Nouvelle Revue Française, 1928.

Clouard, H. *La Destinée tragique de Gérard de Nerval*, Paris, Grasset, 1929.

Coulon, Marcel, *Le Problème de Rimbaud, poète maudit*, Paris, G. Crès, 1923.

Coulon, Marcel, "Les 'Vraies' Lettres du Rimbaud arabo-éthiopien," *Mercure de France*, 15 mars, 1929.

Crise de l'Objet, Paris, Cahiers d'Art, 1936.

Daniel-Rops, Henry, *Les Années tournantes*, Paris, Editions du siècle, Catalogne et Cⁱᵉ, 1932.

Daniel-Rops, Henry, *Rimbaud, le drame spirituel*, Paris, Plon, 1936.

Delahaye, Ernest, *Rimbaud*, Reims, Paris, Revue Littéraire de Paris et de Champagne, 1906.

Dumas, George, *Les Etats intellectuels dans la mélancolie*, Paris, 1895.

Etiemble, Y., *Rimbaud*, Nouvelle Revue Française, 1936.

Franck, Ad., *Nouveaux essais de critique philosophique*, Paris, Hachette, 1890.

Guillemin, Henri, *Le Jocelyn de Lamartine*, Paris, Boivin & Cie, (no date).

Guyau, M. J., *L'Irréligion de l'avenir*, Paris, F. Alcan, 1887.

Haedens, Kleber, *Gérard de Nerval*, Paris, Grasset, 1939.

Hare, Humphrey, *Sketch for a Portrait of Rimbaud*, London, Brendin Publication Co. (1938).

Hazard, Paul, *Quatre Etudes*, New York, Oxford University Press, 1940.

Hazard, Paul, *Avec Victor Hugo en exil*, Paris, Etudes Françaises, 23ᵉ cahier, 1ᵉʳ janvier, 1931.

Hunt, Herbert J., *The Epic in the Nineteenth Century France*, Oxford, Basil Blackwell, 1941.

Hope, M. J., *The Thoughts of Novalis*, London, David Slott, 1891.

Hughes, Randolph, "Vers la contrée du rêve," *Mercure de France*, 1ᵉʳ août, 1939.

Janet, Paul, "Le Spiritualisme français," *Revue des Deux-Mondes,* LXXV.

Janet, Paul, *Principes de métaphysique et de psychologie: leçons professées à la faculté des lettres de Paris* (1888-94), II Paris, Delagrave, 1897.

Janet, Paul, "Philosophie et Religion," *Revue des Deux-Mondes,* LXXXI.

Janet, Paul, *Crise philosophique,* Paris, G. Baillière, 1865.

Kahn, Gustave, *Symbolistes et Décadents,* Paris, Vanier, 1902.

La Harpe, Jean de, *De l'ordre et du hasard,* Université de Neuchâtel, Mémoires, IX, 1936.

Langel, Auguste, "Le Spiritualisme dans la science," *Revue des Deux-Mondes,* LXXXI.

Lemaître, Georges E., *From Cubism to Surrealism in French Literature,* Cambridge, Mass., Harvard University Press, 1941.

Lévêque, C., "La Nouvelle Philosophie de la nature," Revue des Deux-Mondes, LXXXI.

Maritain, Jacques, *Les Frontières de la poésie,* Paris, Le Roseau d'Or, III, Plon, 1927.

Massis, Henri, *Impressions de guerre* (1914-5), Paris, Crès, 1916.

Massis, Henri, *Les Jeunes Gens d'aujourd'hui,* Paris, Plon-Nourrit, 1913.

Ortega, José y Gasset, *The Dehumanization of Art,* (private translation).

Poincaré, Henri, "Conceptions nouvelles de la matière," *Le Matérialisme actuel,* Paris, Flammarion, 1913.

Pommier, Jean, *La Mystique de Baudelaire,* Paris, Belles Lettres, 1932.

Raymond, Marcel, *De Baudelaire au surréalisme, essai sur le mouvement poétique contemporain,* Paris, R. A. Corrêa, 1933.

Reveille, A., "Le Sentiment religieux," *Revue des Deux-Mondes,* LXXXI.

Rivière, J. et Ramon Fernandez, *Moralisme et Littérature,* Paris, R. A. Corrêa, 1932.

Rivière, Jacques, "Reconnaissance à Dada," *Nouvelle Revue Françatse,* 1er août 1920.

Rolland de Renéville, A., "Du temps que les surréalistes avaient raison, *Nouvelle Revue Française,* 1er octobre, 1935.

Rolland de Renéville, A., *Rimbaud le voyant,* Paris, Au Sans Pareil, 1929.

Le Romantisme allemand, Cahiers du Sud, XVI.

Rousseaux, André, *Revue Universelle,* XXVIII.

Ruchon, François, *J. A. Rimbaud,* Paris, Librairie Ancienne Honoré Champion, 1929.

Saint-Pol-Roux, "Autour de la conférence de Camille Mauclair sur Maurice Maeterlinck," *Mercure de France,* juin 1892.

Saint-Pol-Roux, "La Mobilisation de l'imagination," *Mercure de France,* CXX.

Saint-Pol-Roux, "Les Reliefs," *Mercure de France,* II.

Saint-Pol-Roux, "Réponse périe en mer," *Mercure de France,* CIII.

Spenlé, E. *Novalis,* Paris, (no publisher indicated) 1904.

Tancrède de Visan, "Sur l'œuvre de Maurice Maeterlinck," *Vers et Prose,* VIII.

Taupin, René et L. Zukofsky, *Le Style Apollinaire,* Paris, Presses Modernes, 1934.

Thibaudet, Albert, "La Révolution des cinq," *Revue de Paris,* 15 août, 1934.

Thibaudet, Albert, *Le Triptype de la poésie moderne, Verlaine, Rimbaud, Mallarmé,* Causeries Françaises, 2ᵉ année, 2ᵉ causerie, Supplément à la Bibliographie de la France, no. 7, 15 février, 1924.

Trahard, Pierre, *Le Mystère poétique,* Boivin & Cⁱᵉ, 1940.

Truc, Gonzague, *Une Crise intellectuelle,* Paris, Bossard, 1919.

Tzara, Tristan, "Essai sur la situation de la poésie," *Le Surréalisme au Service de la Révolution,* IV.

Vacherot, E. "La Science et la Conscience," *Revue des Deux-Mondes,* LXXXI.

Viatte, Auguste, *Victor Hugo et les Illuminés de son temps,* Montréal, Editions de l'Arbre, 1942.

Wilson, Edmund, *Axel's Castle,* Scribner's, 1935.

Index of Names

This Index includes names of authors, their associates, critics, artists cited, and names of literary movements mentioned. Those page references which are the most important are given in bold type.